AMERICAN POETS PROJECT

AMERICAN POETS PROJECT

IS PUBLISHED WITH A GIFT IN MEMORY OF

James Merrill

AND SUPPORT FROM ITS FOUNDING PATRONS

Sidney J. Weinberg, Jr. Foundation

The Berkley Foundation

Richard B. Fisher and Jeanne Donovan Fisher

John Berryman

selected poems

kevin young editor

AMERICAN POETS PROJECT

THE LIBRARY OF AMERICA

The paper used in this publication meets the minimum requirements of the American National Standard for Information Sciences—Permanence of Paper for Printed Library Materials, ANSI Z39.48—1984.

Design by Chip Kidd and Mark Melnick.
Frontispiece: © Terrence Spencer / Time Life Pictures / Getty Images

Library of Congress Cataloging-in-Publication Data:
Berryman, John, 1914–1972.
  [Poems. Selections]
  Selected poems / John Berryman ; Kevin Young, editor.
    p. cm. — (American poets project ; 11)
  Includes bibliographical references and index.
  ISBN 1–931082–69–3 (alk. paper)
    I. Young, Kevin. II. Title. III. Series.
PS3503.E744A6 2004
811'.54 — dc22
2004048570

10 9 8 7 6 5 4 3 2 1

John
Berryman

CONTENTS

INTRODUCTION

In John Berryman's longer poems, protagonists search for a lover or friend, ancestor or listener with a recklessness that only Whitman allowed himself. But unlike Whitman, or Eliot, Berryman has suffered for his epic impulse: the long, fragmentary form he practiced and in some ways invented does not fit the way we are taught poetry today. Who would rather take a week teaching Berryman's *Dream Songs* than an hour with the self-contained "For the Union Dead" by Robert Lowell or Elizabeth Bishop's "The Fish"? Far harder to explain Berryman's slapstick. When I dare to teach the poems, I find that for every *I don't get it* there are four more *I can't stand it*s and, inevitably, one kid who gets a gleam in her eye, or a smirk on his face, and says nothing —until conferences, when I hear them confess how much they like Berryman.

Like his raucous character Henry, protagonist of *The Dream Songs*, Berryman emerges in his life and work a "human American man." What *The Dream Songs* admits—

meaning both "lets in" and "fesses up to"—including alcoholism, race, sex and sexism, depression, obsession, and desire, makes it the more American. Like many of us, from president to pauper, Berryman presents a host of contradictions: agnostic and believer, agitator and traditionalist, sensitive male and insensitive egoist. Whether he's the craftsman of the early poems, the bon vivant obsessed with death of *The Dream Songs*, or the overconfident boor of the late, uneven *Love & Fame*, Berryman's career reflects his rapid, even frustrating changes. These vertiginous shifts are at the core of why he matters as a poet.

Born John Allyn Smith in 1914 in McAlester, Oklahoma, the future poet moved to Florida with his parents and younger brother shortly after turning 11. In June 1925, his father, whose restaurant business had recently failed, was found shot dead outside their home. His death, which was ruled a suicide (although there were some irregularities in the investigation), haunted Berryman all his life. Echoes of the event taunt Henry in *The Dream Songs*. Berryman's charismatic mother remained a powerful, ambiguous force throughout his life. Born Martha, known as Peggy, she changed her name to "Jill Angel" upon marrying John McAlpin Berryman, mere months after her first husband died. (The boy's new stepfather had been his mother's lover for several months before the fatal incident.) Her son was soon renamed John Allyn McAlpin Berryman and sent to boarding school in Connecticut.

Berryman attended Columbia University, where his poems began to attract attention, winning prizes and appearing in such publications as *The Nation*. As a literary and academic careerist his life was outwardly a success; he forged friendships (and friendly rivalries) with other poets such as Delmore Schwartz and Robert Lowell, taught at Harvard and Princeton before settling into long tenure at the University of Minnesota, published a study of Stephen Crane, and worked at a volume on Shakespeare (never completed, although its existing elements have recently been collected). However, unlike Schwartz or Lowell, Berryman did not achieve poetic success, either in prizes or in poems, until the 1950s.

Indeed, Berryman's earliest poems are a far cry from the staggering, swaggering, intoxicating lines of his greatest works, whether we consider these *The Dream Songs* (or at least the first 77); his *Sonnets*, mostly written in 1947 but not published until 1967; or his first successful long poem, *Homage to Mistress Bradstreet*, first published in 1953. For me, early Berryman at his most compelling approaches what is central in another mid-century Midwesterner, Weldon Kees—a simultaneous strong visual sense and an emptiness as in the best abstract art. I have included in this collection some of Berryman's first poems in order to give a sense of his development, with an eye toward what's to follow in his art and life. In particular the fascinating "Elegy: Hart Crane" foreshadows *Homage to Mistress Bradstreet*—both share the same stilted yet sensuous diction and channeling of a literary ancestor. The poem's ending, with its evocation of Crane's suicide in the Gulf of Mexico and of his epic poem *The Bridge*, hauntingly anticipates Berryman's own suicide decades later, when he jumped off a bridge in Minneapolis.

The Dispossessed (1948), Berryman's first full-length volume of poetry, reveals a large debt to Auden and Yeats; many of the poems have moments of real power and grace. Most remarkable are "The Nervous Songs," a bold series that leads away from the era's dominant idiom toward the agitated, angular, veering style (and flexible form) that Berryman would make his own in the *Sonnets* and *Homage to Mistress Bradstreet* and, most daringly, in *The Dream*

Songs. In their use of personae and of disconnection, "The Nervous Songs" exemplify what Berryman later describes, in the brilliant prose statement "One Answer to a Question: Changes" (1965), as his primary concern: "one personality shifting into another." Throughout his work, the making and unmaking of self can be traced through the fracturings of Berryman's various personae: the poet Anne Bradstreet and the "I" who speaks to her; "Lise," the name he gives to the subject of his *Sonnets*; and, most indelibly, Henry House and his unnamed heckler in *The Dream Songs*.

In *Homage to Mistress Bradstreet*, through the unlikely persona of a 17th-century Puritan poet and a diction at times tortuous in its mix of modern and archaic, Berryman freed himself from derivative modes and from what he called "the Climate," arriving at a tone all his own: a tone mingling artifice and rawness, high and low, as persona and poet confer across time and cultures. Berryman does something akin to Method acting—something psychological, intense, and personal but ultimately performative—breaking decorum and mixing faith with doubt, agape with desire. *Homage* ranks as one of the best long poems of the century, and if he hadn't gone on to write *The Dream Songs* we would still hold him in high regard.

Homage to Mistress Bradstreet was not Berryman's first venture into long poetic projects. The appearance of "Sonnet XXV" in *Poetry* in 1957 and his small but significant collection *His Thought Made Pockets & the Plane Buckt* the following year hinted at a body of work as yet unseen. In 1947 he had written the flurry of sonnets that would be published in 1967 as *Berryman's Sonnets*, a sequence that recounts the beginnings, throes, and aftermath of an adulterous affair. The sonnets, with their merging of archaisms and "gin-&-limes," of lust, daiquiris, self-deception, and a chunk of literary history from Wyatt to Donne, are a heady mix. We can already find the reeling style, the free-wheeling formal invention, the "Crumpling a syntax at a sudden need" that would mark *The Dream Songs*.

As Berryman himself explained it, *The Dream Songs* "is essentially about an imaginary character (not the poet, not me) named Henry, a white American in early middle age sometimes in blackface, who has suffered an irreversible loss and talks about himself sometimes in the first person, sometimes in the third, sometimes even in the second; he has a friend, never named, who addresses him as Mr Bones and variants thereof." The long sequence came out in two separate books—77 *Dream Songs* (1964) and *His Toy, His Dream, His Rest* (1968)—before being collected as a single volume. Winning the National Book Award for *His Toy, His Dream, His Rest*, Berryman revealed in his acceptance speech the influences, temperament, and "gall" that led him to write *The Dream Songs* in the first place:

> Both the writer and the reader of long poems need gall, the outrageous, the intolerable—and they need it again and again. The prospect of ignominious failure must haunt them continually. Whitman, our greatest poet, had all this. Eliot, next, perhaps even greater than Whitman, had it too. Pound makes a marvelous if frail third here. All three dazzlingly original, you notice, and very hostile, both Pound and Eliot, to Whitman. It is no good looking for models. We want anti-models.

In typical Berryman fashion, he saved his bile for critics and for his contemporaries: "I set up the *Dream Songs* as hostile to every visible tendency in both American and English poetry—in so far as the English have any poetry nowadays."

I should say here that my own initial judgment of *The Dream Songs* was harsh and unequivocal: I hated them.

They are difficult, dense, even offensive; the protagonist Henry, while he solicits our empathy, often vexes us. In the *Dream Songs* we are at the mercy, as Henry is, of fantasy—of women, of death, of drink. If indeed dreams, the poems seem to emerge out of the restless boozy sleep of the alcoholic, full of fits and starts; they provide an odd mix of "scrambling, sitting, spattering" rhythm and underlying monotone. I cannot say what transformation made me laugh with them instead of at them, or stop worrying that Berryman was laughing at me as reader—it helped to realize that the joke was cosmic. Once I did, I saw how, in going along with Berryman, we are not so much the priest privy to confession as we are (as Helen Vendler has convincingly argued) the silent therapist listening to the analysand's rantings. But most often, we are the audience captive to the poet's mesmerizing performance, in equal parts seduced by and coerced into collusion with the poetry, laughing uneasily with Berryman at death or fate or desires that had always seemed unspeakable. Not a comfortable vantage as reader, but one that revels in the gall that the writing itself demands.

Perhaps I got past my initial resistance to *The Dream Songs* because I'm a sucker for poems that may best be called "successful failures"—those overreaching, underplanned, unruly, wonderful messes that do not aspire to formal perfection but delight with their sense of surprise, of *personality*. Their failure, if it can be called that, is not of imagination but of eyes too big for the stomach; they may even be said to mirror more exactly our modern world. *The Dream Songs*, in fact, courts failure; the prospect of defeat haunts the poems as much as the ghost of Berryman's suicide father. Often he takes failure as his explicit subject: "The reason I don't do this more (I quote)/is: I have a living to fail—//because of my wife & son—to keep from earning." The disappointments that Henry experiences become a sign of honor and source of humor, a red badge of cowardice, a set of admissions that

> Life, friends, is boring. We must not say so.
> After all, the sky flashes, the great sea yearns,
> we ourselves flash and yearn,
> and moreover my mother told me as a boy
> (repeatingly) 'Ever to confess you're bored
> means you have no
>
> Inner Resources.' I conclude now I have no
> inner resources, because I am heavy bored.
> Peoples bore me,
> literature bores me, especially great literature,
> Henry bores me, with his plights & gripes
> as bad as achilles . . .

The passage, layered with wicked ironies beneath the surface ennui, shows Berryman's characteristic willingness to make fun of literature in a poem that nevertheless seeks greatness. Along with the echoes of Greek epic, Berryman gives us come-ons, bar-talk, braggadocio ("My psychiatrist can lick your psychiatrist"), radio chatter: in short, everything filtering through his mind, as well as through a certain American subconscious. Indeed, what ultimately fails may not be Henry, but the same American dream that named Langston Hughes' *Montage of a Dream Deferred.*

However subconscious their feel, *The Dream Songs* are certainly willed and conscious in their effect on the page. Indeed, *The Dream Songs* are play-acted: Berryman creates an on-stage double for a vaudeville of race, mock tragedy, and harsh comedy. Not only is Henry a mask, however thin, for Berryman, the poem itself is a kind of *masque*— elaborate, mannered pageantry. The power of the poems comes not from revealing the poet bare-faced or naked but from maintaining the mask (or many) even in the face of despair. The poem must go on, and on it does, pal, its forward motion providing (or mimicking) an antidote to despair just as the voice shifts between "you" and "I," high and low, archaic language and contemporary slang.

Included in that mix are hints of the blues music that Berryman loved. He is at his best not when he attempts to write directly about the blues (as in Dream Song 68 about Bessie Smith) but when he captures something of their tone, humor, and ironic survival: "I'm scared a lonely." For Berryman, as for many white rock 'n' roll artists, black dialect (however imaginary) provides a gateway to a wider sense of American language, not as a sign of cultural decay but of cultural vitality. The fearlessness with which Berryman breaks through the polite diction of academic poetry into a liberating variety of idioms is a major part of his legacy. If Henry is "a monoglot of English/(American Version)," then Henry's blackface Mr Bones persona—a mask upon a mask—allows him to speak in dialect to reflect on his condition: "He stared at ruin. Ruin stared straight back./He thought they was old friends." Meanwhile, Henry's "friend," ever unnamed—and *not* called Mr Bones, who is in fact Henry himself—provides a running, heckling commentary. In minstrelsy terms, Henry's friend is the Interlocutor, traditionally responsible for the pacing of the minstrel show (and typically the "straight man," not in blackface); in terms of the poem, the on-stage Interlocutor serves to speed things up or slow them down, even to put Henry down, second-guessing his aimless quest.

Much of the force of *The Dream Songs* comes from its use of race and blackface to express a (white) self unraveling. Berryman explores the "blackness" of whiteness in a way I have come to admire—even if, from another angle, he might be said to replicate in all too familiar a fashion the constant use of blackness by whites to say the unsayable. The fact that he does so by using the dead convention of black dialect, derived more from blackface minstrelsy than from actual black life, calls to mind what Ralph Ellison, a friend of Berryman's, wrote about blackface: "Here another ironic facet of the old American problem of identity crops up. For out of the counterfeiting of the black American's identity there arises a profound doubt in the white man's mind as to the authenticity of his own image of himself." It is arguably this doubt that Berryman wants to show us through the phantom imaginings of an onstage, enraged Henry: blackface makes symbolic the "deracination" that Henry feels, the "irreversible loss" that remains unnamed but no less haunting than his Interlocutor and friend. Indeed, loss and ruin and despair and death are "old friends" of Henry's—and however their metaphoric blackness may be troubling, there is an honesty, or at least self-consciousness, about such troubles that poets of all stripes have come to admire, even if, as Michael S. Harper suggests in his poem "Tongue-Tied in Black and White," Berryman himself really did not gauge the extent to which "only your inner voices/spoke such tongues . . . /your ear lied."

After *The Dream Songs* came the starkly forthright collection *Love & Fame*, in which Berryman seemed to have discarded the mask entirely—indeed, to have erased the line, however faint or blurry, that *The Dream Songs* drew between art and autobiography. The book's reviews ranged from tepid to savage, and there was some queasiness about Berryman's reveling in the bad behavior of his past. However ironic the book's title was meant to be, that a prize-winning professor-poet could present such a bald account of his desires was more than some readers, or even Berryman, could bear; he expunged several poems from the second edition.

At the end of the volume appeared "Eleven Addresses to the Lord," which marks the beginning of the religious poetry of Berryman's last phase, continuing in the opening "Opus Dei" sequence of his final book, *Delusions, Etc.* In many ways, his work came full circle: if his middle, elegiac period, including the *Sonnets* and *His Thought*, is most in need of rediscovery, then these late poems are most in need of redemption. In the proof stage when he committed suicide in January 1972, *Delusions* serves as a kind of summing up. We have here the poignant last lines of "He Resigns," and the triumphant strangeness of his poem to Emily Dickinson, "Your Birthday in Wisconsin You Are 140." "Hot diggity!" the poem declares with an exuberance many of the poems share. The book included two additional Dream Songs; the last, "Henry's Understanding," is haunting for its plainspoken certainty: ". . . it occurred to me/that *one* night, instead of warm pajamas,/I'd take off all my clothes/& cross the damp cold lawn & down the bluff/ into the terrible water & walk forever/under it out toward the island."

In recalling this earlier suicidal thought, Berryman seems to be calling his own bluff, forecasting what would follow: before the book was published, he would take his life by jumping off a bridge. Legend is, he waved.

Kevin Young
August 2004

Note on E. A. Robinson

He was forever walking
A little north
To watch the bare words stalking
Stiffly forth,
Frozen as they went
And flawless of heart within, without comment.

Elegy: Hart Crane

I

Secure and white the shroud about the head,
The imperceptible sea rests on his brow
And salt is where the lips. Question the dead
Does not disturb, is not insistent now.

Let his design—immense immaculate curve
Set upon rock and shouldered by the tide
Gainless against the base—that span deserve
Another architect, and sea decide.

For here the hand was water when above
The mother task was difficult and slow,
The cables wave-suspended: until his love
Saw towers bend with desire and rivets flow.

And subtle as the sifting of the will
Like sand into the years, return was there:
The promise and the lover and the still
Serene unfathomed altar of his prayer.

II

Impermanence in place, he will not walk
Again the swift contemporary sky
And watch the buildings wheel below and talk
Chaos as wind and stone condemned to eye.

No longer symbol star and the tall steel
Unbalance poise, drop hovering winded heart
Down corridors of man where kestrels reel
Resistless to the vortex, and depart.

That scrutiny is skilled now to regard
The minute shifting of the water's floor
As once the wheeling eye was high and hard
Over the vast palimpsest of the shore.

As had the ear heard loud and long on land
Train thunder, throated cry and the great bell
Of evening earth, there now concern with sand
Whispers of purple anemone and shell.

O mourn the legend left here in the first
Full sun, fragments of light to tell the day.
Tread slowly, softly silence while the dust
Whirls up the sky and walls the sound away.

Cantlets of speech: beyond the reach of light
Beyond all architecture, the last ledge,
He is obscure in ocean in the night—
Monstrous and still, brooding above the bridge.

The Second Cactus

Gifts are a peg on which to hang repose,
On which to hang delight and hope it stays;
Lost, fallen out, death after holiday.

Man is the ground of many deaths, the small
The darkest, deep, terrible to recall,
An end to sleep and more than we can pay.

In March I failed to water what you gave
And on my mantel it found a dry grave,
The beard grew white, the body thin and grey.

Now, as not often in this nightmare place,
The shut lost door opens again, in case
I change, can shovel that grave quite away.

Prague

(Voice and Echo)

The crowd like silence. Do they await there death?
> *Their death.*

Why does this people suddenly shout, break?
> *Outbreak.*

And are they murdered by their own battalion?
> *Alien.*

Which guns so rapidly can conjure men?
> *German.*

What symbol justifies this consternation?
> *Nation.*

Will the Leader do anything but charm them?
> *Arm them.*

And on what level does that man set Reason?
> *Treason.*

But what succeeds to all this banner-shaking?
> *Aching.*

Shall we cross, interfere across an ocean?
> *No, shun.*

Then what have we to do with that Power, Fear?
> *Our fear.*

The Apparition

Frequently when the night
Binds Austria and England in
One indiscriminate place,
Staring I see between
A familiar chair and the slight
Smile of a fresco god your face.

Which from the advancing eye
Withdraws, miles in an instant,
Is quite gone, and the god
Resumes his banishment
To curtain mathematics: dry
And bitter the brain is in my head.

Could I suspend sight where
It met you, could I command
Instinct be still, blood still,
I fancy you might stand
And your eyes, even your hair
Stay to reward that skill.

Tonight I will do: patience
Rule my long love and guide
The wild nerves when they start.
But something will have died
From me if I look once
There and restrain my heart.

Cambridge
1937

The Curse

Cedars and the westward sun.
The darkening sky. A man alone
Watches beside the fallen wall
The evening multitudes of sin
Crowd in upon us all.
For when the light fails they begin
Nocturnal sabotage among
The outcast and the loose of tongue,
The lax in walk, the murderers:
Our twilight universal curse.

Children are faultless in the wood,
Untouched. If they are later made
Scandal and index to their time,
It is that twilight brings for bread
The faculty of crime.
Only the idiot and the dead
Stand by, while who were young before
Wage insolent and guilty war
By night within that ancient house,
Immense, black, damned, anonymous.

To Bhain Campbell

1911–1940

I told a lie once in a verse. I said
I said I said I said 'The heart will mend,
Body will break and mend, the foam replace
For even the unconsolable his taken friend.'
This is a lie. I had not been here then.

Epilogue

He died in December. He must descend
Somewhere, vague and cold, the spirit and seal,
The gift descend, and all that insight fail
Somewhere. Imagination one's one friend
Cannot see there. Both of us at the end.
Nouns, verbs do not exist for what I feel.

Winter Landscape

The three men coming down the winter hill
In brown, with tall poles and a pack of hounds
At heel, through the arrangement of the trees,
Past the five figures at the burning straw,
Returning cold and silent to their town,

Returning to the drifted snow, the rink
Lively with children, to the older men,
The long companions they can never reach,
The blue light, men with ladders, by the church
The sledge and shadow in the twilit street,

Are not aware that in the sandy time
To come, the evil waste of history
Outstretched, they will be seen upon the brow
Of that same hill: when all their company
Will have been irrecoverably lost,

These men, this particular three in brown
Witnessed by birds will keep the scene and say
By their configuration with the trees,
The small bridge, the red houses and the fire,
What place, what time, what morning occasion

Sent them into the wood, a pack of hounds
At heel and the tall poles upon their shoulders,
Thence to return as now we see them and
Ankle-deep in snow down the winter hill
Descend, while three birds watch and the fourth flies.

The Traveller

They pointed me out on the highway, and they said
'That man has a curious way of holding his head.'

They pointed me out on the beach; they said 'That man
Will never become as we are, try as he can.'

They pointed me out at the station, and the guard
Looked at me twice, thrice, thoughtfully & hard.

I took the same train that the others took,
To the same place. Were it not for that look
And those words, we were all of us the same.
I studied merely maps. I tried to name
The effects of motion on the travellers,
I watched the couple I could see, the curse
And blessings of that couple, their destination,
The deception practised on them at the station,
Their courage. When the train stopped and they knew
The end of their journey, I descended too.

The Ball Poem

What is the boy now, who has lost his ball,
What, what is he to do? I saw it go
Merrily bouncing, down the street, and then
Merrily over—there it is in the water!
No use to say 'O there are other balls':
An ultimate shaking grief fixes the boy
As he stands rigid, trembling, staring down
All his young days into the harbour where
His ball went. I would not intrude on him,
A dime, another ball, is worthless. Now
He senses first responsibility
In a world of possessions. People will take balls,
Balls will be lost always, little boy,
And no one buys a ball back. Money is external.
He is learning, well behind his desperate eyes,
The epistemology of loss, how to stand up
Knowing what every man must one day know
And most know many days, how to stand up
And gradually light returns to the street,
A whistle blows, the ball is out of sight,
Soon part of me will explore the deep and dark
Floor of the harbour . . I am everywhere,
I suffer and move, my mind and my heart move
With all that move me, under the water
Or whistling, I am not a little boy.

Parting as Descent

The sun rushed up the sky; the taxi flew;
There was a kind of fever on the clock
That morning. We arrived at Waterloo
With time to spare and couldn't find my track.

The bitter coffee in a small café
Gave us our conversation. When the train
Began to move, I saw you turn away
And vanish, and the vessels in my brain

Burst, the train roared, the other travellers
In flames leapt, burning on the tilted air
Che si cruccia, I heard the devils curse
And shriek with joy in that place beyond prayer.

Letter to His Brother

The night is on these hills, and some can sleep.
Some stare into the dark, some walk.
Only the sound of glasses and of talk,
Of cracking logs, and of a few who weep,
Comes on the night wind to my waking ears.
Your enemies and mine are still,
None works upon us either good or ill:
Mint by the stream, tree-frogs, are travellers.

What shall I say for anniversary?
At Dachau rubber blows forbid
And Becket's brains upon the pavement spread
Forbid my trust, my hopeful prophecy.
Prediction if I make, I violate
The just expectancy of youth,—
Although you know as well as I whose tooth
Sunk in our heels, the western guise of fate.

When Patrick Barton chased the murderer
He heard behind him in the wood
Pursuit, and suddenly he knew hé fled:
He was the murderer, the others were
His vigilance. But when he crouched behind
A tree, the tree moved off and left
Him naked while the cry came on; he laughed
And like a hound he leapt out of his mind.

I wish for you—the moon was full, is gone—
Whatever bargain can be got
From the violent world our fathers bought,
For which we pay with fantasy at dawn,
Dismay at noon, fatigue, horror by night.
May love, or its image in work,
Bring you the brazen luck to sleep with dark
And so to get responsible delight.

1938

The Animal Trainer (1)

I told him: The time has come, I must be gone.
It is time to leave the circus and circus days,
The admissions, the menagerie, the drums,
Excitements of disappointment and praise.
In a suburb of the spirit I shall seize
The steady and exalted light of the sun,
And live there, out of the tension that decays,
Until I become a man alone of noon.

Heart said: Can you do without your animals?
The looking, licking, smelling animals?
The friendly fumbling beast? The listening one?
That standing up and worst of animals?
What will become of you in the pure light
When all your enemies are gone, and gone
The inexhaustible prospect of the night?

—But the night is now the body of my fear,
These animals are my distraction. Once
Let me escape the smells and cages here,
Once let me stand naked in the sun,
All these performances will be forgotten.
I shall concentrate in the sunlight there.

Said the conservative Heart: Your animals
Are occupation, food for you, your love
And your immense responsibility;
They are the travellers by which you live.
(Without you they will pace and pine, or die.)

—I reared them, tended them (I said) and still
They plague me, they will not perform, they run
Into forbidden corners, they fight, they steal.
Better to live like an artist in the sun.

—You are an animal trainer, Heart replied.
Without your animals leaping at your side
No sun will save you, nor this bloodless pride.

—What must I do then? Must I stay and work
With animals, and confront the night, in the circus?

—You léarn from animals. You léarn in the dark.

The Animal Trainer (2)

I told him: The time has come, I must be gone.
It is time to leave the circus and circus days,
The admissions, the menagerie, the drums,
Excitements of disappointment and praise.
In a suburb of the spirit I shall seize
The steady and exalted light of the sun
And live there, out of the tension that decays,
Until I become a man alone of noon.

Heart said: Can you do without these animals?
The looking, licking, smelling animals?
The friendly fumbling beast? The listening one?
The standing up and worst of animals?

What will become of you in the pure light
When all your enemies are gone, and gone
The inexhaustible prospect of the night?

—But the night is now the body of my fear,
These animals are my distraction! Once
Let me escape the smells and cages here,
Once let me stand naked in the sun,
All their performances will be forgotten.
I shall concentrate in the sunlight there.

Said the conservative Heart: These animals
Are occupation, food for you, your love
And your despair, responsibility:
They are the travellers by which you live.
Without you they will pace and pine, or die.

—What soul-delighting tasks do they perform?
They quarrel, snort, leap, lie down, their delight
Merely a punctual meal and to be warm.
Justify their existence in the night!

—The animals are coupling, and they cry
'The circus *is*, it is our mystery,
It is a world of dark where animals die.'

—Animals little and large, be still, be still:
I'll stay with you. Suburb and sun are pale.

—Animals are your destruction, and your will.

1 September 1939

The first, scattering rain on the Polish cities.
That afternoon a man squat' on the shore
Tearing a square of shining cellophane.
Some easily, some in evident torment tore,
Some for a time resisted, and then burst.
All this depended on fidelity . .
One was blown out and borne off by the waters,
The man was tortured by the sound of rain.

Children were sent from London in the morning
But not the sound of children reached his ear.
He found a mangled feather by the lake,
Lost in the destructive sand this year
Like feathery independence, hope. His shadow
Lay on the sand before him, under the lake
As under the ruined library our learning.
The children play in the waves until they break.

The Bear crept under the Eagle's wing and lay
Snarling; the other animals showed fear,
Europe darkened its cities. The man wept,
Considering the light which had been there,
The feathered gull against the twilight flying.
As the little waves ate away the shore
The cellophane, dismembered, blew away.
The animals ran, the Eagle soared and dropt.

The Moon and the Night and the Men

On the night of the Belgian surrender the moon rose
Late, a delayed moon, and a violent moon
For the English or the American beholder;
The French beholder. It was a cold night,
People put on their wraps, the troops were cold
No doubt, despite the calendar, no doubt
Numbers of refugees coughed, and the sight
Or sound of some killed others. A cold night.

On Outer Drive there was an accident:
A stupid well-intentioned man turned sharp
Right and abruptly he became an angel
Fingering an unfamiliar harp,
Or screamed in hell, or was nothing at all.
Do not imagine this is unimportant.
He was a part of the night, part of the land,
Part of the bitter and exhausted ground
Out of which memory grows.

                              Michael and I
Stared at each other over chess, and spoke
As little as possible, and drank and played.
The chessmen caught in the European eye,
Neither of us I think had a free look
Although the game was fair. The move one made
It was difficult at last to keep one's mind on.
'Hurt and unhappy' said the man in London.
We said to each other, The time is coming near
When none shall have books or music, none his dear,
And only a fool will speak aloud his mind.

History is approaching a speechless end,
As Henry Adams said. Adams was right.

All this occurred on the night when Leopold
Fulfilled the treachery four years before
Begun—or was he well-intentioned, more
Roadmaker to hell than king? At any rate,
The moon came up late and the night was cold,
Many men died—although we know the fate
Of none, nor of anyone, and the war
Goes on, and the moon in the breast of man is cold.

A Poem for Bhain

Although the relatives in the summer house
Gossip and grumble, do what relatives do,
Demand, demand our eyes and ears, demand us,

You and I are not precisely there
As they require: heretics, we converse
Alert and alone, as over a lake of fire

Two white birds following their profession
Of flight, together fly, loom, fall and rise,
Certain of the nature and station of their mission.

So by the superficial and summer lake
We talk, and nothing that we say is heard,
Neither by the relatives who twitter and ache

Nor by any traveller nor by any bird.

Canto Amor

Dream in a dream the heavy soul somewhere
struck suddenly & dark down to its knees.
A griffin sighs off in the orphic air.

If (Unknown Majesty) I not confess
praise for the wrack the rock the live sailor
under the blue sea,—yet I may You bless

always for hér, in fear & joy for hér
whose gesture summons ever when I grieve
me back and is my mage and minister.

—Muses: whose worship I may never leave
but for this pensive woman, now I dare,
teach me her praise! with her my praise receive.—

Three years already of the round world's war
had rolled by stoned & disappointed eyes
when she and I came where we were made for.

Pale as a star lost in returning skies,
more beautiful than midnight stars more frail
she moved towards me like chords, a sacrifice;

entombed in body trembling through the veil
arm upon arm, learning our ancient wound,
we see our one soul heal, recovering pale.

Then priestly sanction, then the drop of sound.
Quickly part to the cavern ever warm
deep from the march, body to body bound,

descend (my soul) out of dismantling storm
into the darkness where the world is made.
. . Come back to the bright air. Love is multiform.

Heartmating hesitating unafraid
although incredulous, she seemed to fill
the lilac shadow with light wherein she played,

whom sorry childhood had made sit quite still,
an orphan silence, unregarded sheen,
listening for any small soft note, not hopeful:

caricature: as once a maiden Queen,
flowering power comeliness kindness grace,
shattered her mirror, wept, would not be seen.

These pities moved. Also above her face
serious or flushed, swayed her fire-gold
not earthly hair, now moonless to unlace,

resistless flame, now in a sun more cold
great shells to whorl about each secret ear,
mysterious histories, white shores, unfold.

New musics! One the music that we hear,
this is the music which the masters make
out of their minds, profound solemn & clear.

And then the other music, in whose sake
all men perceive a gladness but we are drawn
less for that joy than utterly to take

our trial, naked in the music's vision,
the flowing ceremony of trouble and light,
all Loves becoming, none to flag upon.

Such Mozart made,—an ear so delicate
he fainted at a trumpet-call, a child
so delicate. So merciful that sight,

so stern, we follow rapt who ran a-wild.
Marriage is the second music, and thereof
we hear what we can bear, faithful & mild.

Therefore the streaming torches in the grove
through dark or bright, swiftly & now more near
cherish a festival of anxious love.

Dance for this music, Mistress to music dear,
more, that storm worries the disordered wood
grieving the midnight of my thirtieth year

and only the trial of our music should
still this irresolute air, only your voice
spelling the tempest may compel our good:

Sigh then beyond my song: whirl & rejoice!

The Song of the Demented Priest

I put those things there.—See them burn.
The emerald the azure and the gold
Hiss and crack, the blues & greens of the world
As if I were tired. Someone interferes
Everywhere with me. The clouds, the clouds are torn
In ways I do not understand or love.

Licking my long lips, I looked upon God
And he flamed and he was friendlier
Than you were, and he was small. Showing me
Serpents and thin flowers; these were cold.
Dominion waved & glittered like the flare
From ice under a small sun. I wonder.

Afterward the violent and formal dancers
Came out, shaking their pithless heads.
I would instruct them but I cannot now,—
Because of the elements. They rise and move,
I nod a dance and they dance in the rain
In my red coat. I am the king of the dead.

A Professor's Song

(. . rabid or dog-dull.) Let me tell you how
The Eighteenth Century couplet ended. Now
Tell me. Troll me the sources of that Song—
Assigned last week—by Blake. Come, come along,
Gentlemen. (Fidget and huddle, do. Squint soon.)
I want to end these fellows all by noon.

'That deep romantic chasm'—an early use;
The word is from the French, by our abuse
Fished out a bit. (Red all your eyes. O when?)
'A poet is a man speaking to men':
But I am then a poet, am I not?—
Ha ha. The radiator, please. Well, what?

Alive now—no—Blake would have written prose,
But movement following movement crisply flows,
So much the better, better the much so,
As burbleth Mozart. Twelve. The class can go.
Until I meet you, then, in Upper Hell
Convulsed, foaming immortal blood: farewell.

The Song of the Tortured Girl

After a little I could not have told—
But no one asked me this—why I was there.
I asked. The ceiling of that place was high
And there were sudden noises, which I made.
I must have stayed there a long time today:
My cup of soup was gone when they brought me back.

Often "Nothing worse now can come to us"
I thought, the winter the young men stayed away,
My uncle died, and mother broke her crutch.
And then the strange room where the brightest light
Does not shine on the strange men: shines on me.
I feel them stretch my youth and throw a switch.

Through leafless branches the sweet wind blows
Making a mild sound, softer than a moan;
High in a pass once where we put our tent,
Minutes I lay awake to hear my joy.
—I no longer remember what they want.—
Minutes I lay awake to hear my joy.

A Winter-Piece to a Friend Away

Your letter came.—Glutted the earth & cold
With rains long heavy, follows intense frost;
    Snow howls and hides the world
We workt awhile to build; all the roads are lost;
Icy spiculae float, filling strange air;
No voice goes far; one is alone whirling since where,
    And when was it one crossed?
    You have been there.

I too the breaking blizzard's eddies bore
One year, another year: tempted to drop
    At my own feet forlorn
Under the warm fall, frantic more to chop
Wide with the gale until my thought ran numb
Clenching the blue skin tight against what white spikes
    come,
    And the sick brain estop.
    Your pendulum

Mine, not stilled wholly, has been sorry for,
Weeps from, and would instruct . . Unless I lied
    What word steadies that cord?
Glade grove & ghyll of antique childhood glide
Off; from our grown grief, weathers that appal,
The massive sorrow of the mental hospital,
    Friends & our good friends hide.
    They came to call.

Hardly theirs, moment when the tempest gains,
Loose heart convulses. Their hearts bend off dry,
    Their fruit dangles and fades.
—Solicitudes of the orchard heart, comply
A little with my longing, a little sing
Our sorrow among steel & glass, our stiffening,
    That hers may modify:
    O trembling Spring.—

Immortal risks our sort run, to a house
Reported in a wood . . mould upon bread
    And brain, breath giving out,
From farms we go by, barking, and shaken head,
The shrunk pears hang, Hölderlin's weathercock
Rattles to tireless wind, the fireless landscape rock,
    Artists insane and dead
    Strike like a clock:

If the fruit is dead, fast. Wait. Chafe your left wrist.
All these too lie, whither a true form strays.
    Sweet when the lost arrive.
Foul sleet ices the twigs, the vision frays,
Festoons all signs; still as I come to name
My joy to you my joy springs up again the same,—
    The thaw alone delays,—
    Your letter came!

New Year's Eve

The grey girl who had not been singing stopped,
And a brave new no-sound blew through acrid air.
I set my drink down, hard. Somebody slapped
Somebody's second wife somewhere,
Wheeling away to long to be alone.
I see the dragon of years is almost done,
Its claws loosen, its eyes
Crust now with tears & lust and a scale of lies.

A whisky-listless and excessive saint
Was expounding his position, whom I hung
Boy-glad in glowing heaven: he grows faint:
Hearing what song the sirens sung,
Sidelong he web-slid and some rich prose spun.
The tissue golden of the gifts undone
Surpassed the gifts. Miss Weirs
Whispers to me her international fears.

Intelligentsia milling. In a semi-German
(Our loss of Latin fractured how far our fate,—
Disinterested once, linkage once like a sermon)
I struggle to articulate
Why it is our promise breaks in pieces early.
The Muses' visitants come soon, go surly
With liquor & mirrors away
In this land wealthy & casual as a holiday.

Whom the Bitch winks at. Most of us are linsey-
woolsey workmen, grandiose, and slack.

On m'analyse, the key to secrets. Kinsey
Shortly will tell us sharply back
Habits we stuttered. How revive to join
(Great evils grieve beneath : eye Caesar's coin)
And lure a while more home
The vivid wanderers, uneasy with our shame?

Priests of the infinite! ah, not for long.
The dove whispers, and diminishes
Up the blue leagues. And no doubt we heard wrong—
Wax of our lives collects & dulls; but was
What we heard hurried as we memorized,
Or brightened, or adjusted? Undisguised
We pray our tongues & fingers
Record the strange word that blows suddenly and
       lingers.

Imagine a patience in the works of love
Luck sometimes visits. Ages we have sighed,
And cleave more sternly to a music of
Even this sore word 'genocide'.
Each to his own! Clockless & thankless dream
And labour Makers, being what we seem.
Soon soon enough we turn
Our tools in; brownshirt Time chiefly our works will
       burn.

I remember: white fine flour everywhere whirled
Ceaselessly, wheels rolled, a slow thunder boomed,
And there were snowy men in the mill-world
With sparkling eyes, light hair uncombed,

And one of them was humming an old song,
Sack upon sack grew portly, until strong
Arms moved them on, by pairs,
And then the bell clanged and they ran like hares.

Scotch in his oxter, my Retarded One
Blows in before the midnight; freezing slush
Stamps off, off. Worst of years! . . no matter, begone;
Your slash and spells (in the sudden hush)
We see now we had to suffer some day, so
I cross the dragon with a blessing, low,
While the black blood slows. Clock-wise,
We clasp upon the stroke, kissing with happy cries.

Of 1947

[*Born 1612 Anne Dudley, married at 16 Simon Bradstreet, a Cambridge man, steward to the Countess of Warwick & protégé of her father Thomas Dudley secretary to the Earl of Lincoln. Crossed in the* Arbella, *1630, under Governor Winthrop.*]

. . . 1

The Governor your husband lived so long
moved you not, restless, waiting for him? Still,
you were a patient woman.—
I seem to see you pause here still:
Sylvester, Quarles, in moments odd you pored
before a fire at, bright eyes on the Lord,
all the children still.
'Simon . .' Simon will listen while you read a Song.

. . . 2

Outside the New World winters in grand dark
white air lashing high thro' the virgin stands
foxes down foxholes sigh,
surely the English heart quails, stunned.
I doubt if Simon than this blast, that sea,
spares from his rigour for your poetry
more. We are on each other's hands
who care. Both of our worlds unhanded us. Lie stark,

. . . 3

thy eyes look to me mild. Out of maize & air
your body's made, and moves. I summon, see,
from the centuries it.

I think you won't stay. How do we
linger, diminished, in our lovers' air,
implausibly visible, to whom, a year,
years, over interims; or not;
to a long stranger; or not; shimmer & disappear.

4

Jaw-ript, rot with its wisdom, rending then;
then not. When the mouth dies, who misses you?
Your master never died,
Simon ah thirty years past you—
Pockmarkt & westward staring on a haggard deck
it seems I find you, young. I come to check,
I come to stay with you,
and the Governor, & Father, & Simon, & the huddled men.

By the week we landed we were, most, used up.
Strange ships across us, after a fortnight's winds
unfavouring, frightened us;
bone-sad cold, sleet, scurvy; so were ill
many as one day we could have no sermons;
broils, quelled; a fatherless child unkennelled; vermin
crowding & waiting: waiting.
And the day itself he leapt ashore young Henry Winthrop

(delivered from the waves; because he found
off their wigwams, sharp-eyed, a lone canoe
across a tidal river,
that water glittered fair & blue
& narrow, none of the other men could swim

and the plantation's prime theft up to him,
shouldered on a glad day
hard on the glorious feasting of thanksgiving) drowned.

. . . 7

How long with nothing in the ruinous heat,
clams & acorns stomaching, distinction perishing,
at which my heart rose,
with brackish water, we would sing.
When whispers knew the Governor's last bread
was browning in his oven, we were discourag'd.
The Lady Arbella dying—
dyings—at which my heart   rose, but I did submit.

. . . 8

That beyond the Atlantic wound our woes enlarge
is hard, hard that starvation burnishes our fear,
but I do gloss for You.
Strangers & pilgrims fare we here,
declaring we seek a City. Shall we be deceived?
I know whom I have trusted, & whom I have believed,
and that he is able to
keep   that I have committed to his charge.

. . . 9

Winter than summer worse, that first, like a file
on a quick, or the poison suck of a thrilled tooth;
and still we may unpack.
Wolves & storms among, uncouth
board-pieces, boxes, barrels vanish, grow
houses, rise. Motes that hop in sunlight slow

indoors, and I am Ruth
away: open my mouth, my eyes wet: I wóuld smile:

. . . 10

vellum I palm, and dream. Their forest dies
to greensward, privets, elms & towers, whence
a nightingale is throbbing.
Women sleep sound. I was happy once . .
(Something keeps on not happening; I shrink?)
These minutes all their passions & powers sink
and I am not one chance
for an unknown cry or a flicker of unknown eyes.

. . . 11

Chapped souls ours, by the day Spring's strong winds
        swelled,
Jack's pulpits arched, more glad. The shawl I pinned
flaps like a shooting soul
might in such weather Heaven send.
Succumbing half, in spirit, to a salmon sash
I prod the nerveless novel succotash—
I must be disciplined,
in arms, against that one, and our dissidents, and myself.

. . . 12

Versing, I shroud among the dynasties;
quaternion on quaternion, tireless I phrase
anything past, dead, far,
sacred, for a barbarous place.
—To please your wintry father? all this bald
abstract didactic rime I read appalled

harassed for your fame
mistress neither of fiery nor velvet verse, on your knees

. . . 13

hopeful & shamefast, chaste, laborious, odd,
whom the sea tore.—The damned roar with loss,
so they hug & are mean
with themselves, and I cannot be thus.
Why then do I repine, sick, bad, to long
after what must not be? I lie wrong
once more. For at fourteen
I found my heart more carnal and sitting loose from God,

. . . 14

vanity & the follies of youth took hold of me;
then the pox blasted, when the Lord returned.
That year for my sorry face
so-much-older Simon burned,
so Father smiled, with love. Their will be done.
He to me ill lingeringly, learning to shun
a bliss, a lightning blood
vouchsafed, what did seem life. I kissed his Mystery.

. . . 15

Drydust in God's eye the aquavivid skin
of Simon snoring lit with fountaining dawn
when my eyes unlid, sad.
John Cotton shines on Boston's sin—
I ám drawn, in pieties that seem
the weary drizzle of an unremembered dream.
Women have gone mad
at twenty-one. Ambition mines, atrocious, in.

16

Food endless, people few, all to be done.
As pippins roast, the question of the wolves
turns & turns.
Fangs of a wolf will keep, the neck
round of a child, that child brave. I remember who
in meeting smiled & was punisht, and I know who
whispered & was stockt.
We lead a thoughtful life. But Boston's cage we shun.

The winters close, Springs open, no child stirs
under my withering heart, O seasoned heart
God grudged his aid.
All things else soil like a shirt.
Simon is much away. My executive stales.
The town came through for the cartway by the pales,
but my patience is short.
I revolt from, I am like, these savage foresters

whose passionless dicker in the shade, whose glance
impassive & scant, belie their murderous cries
when quarry seems to show.
Again I must have been wrong, twice.
Unwell in a new way. Can that begin?
God brandishes. O love, O I love. Kin,
gather. My world is strange
and merciful, ingrown months, blessing a swelling
          trance.

19

So squeezed, wince you I scream? I love you & hate
off with you. Ages! *Useless.* Below my waist
he has me in Hell's vise.
Stalling. He let go. Come back: brace
me somewhere. No. No. Yes! everything down
hardens I press with horrible joy down
my back cracks like a wrist
shame I am voiding oh behind it is too late

hide me forever I work thrust I must free
now I all muscles & bones concentrate
what is living from dying?
Simon I must leave you so untidy
Monster you are killing me Be sure
I'll have you later Women do endure
I can *can* no longer
and it passes the wretched trap whelming and I am me

drencht & powerful, I did it with my body!
One proud tug greens Heaven. Marvellous,
unforbidding Majesty.
Swell, imperious bells. I fly.
Mountainous, woman not breaks and will bend:
sways God nearby: anguish comes to an end.
Blossomed Sarah, and I
blossom. Is that thing alive? I hear a famisht howl.

22

Beloved household, I am Simon's wife,
and the mother of Samuel—whom greedy yet I miss
out of his kicking place.
More in some ways I feel at a loss,
freer. Cantabanks & mummers, nears
longing for you. Our chopping scores my ears,
our costume bores my eyes.
St. George to the good sword, rise! chop-logic's rife

& fever & Satan & Satan's ancient fere.
Pioneering is not feeling well,
not Indians, beasts.
Not all their riddling can forestall
one leaving. Sam, your uncle has had to
go fróm us to live with God. 'Then Aunt went too?'
Dear, she does wait still.
Stricken: 'Oh. Then he takes   us one by one.' My dear.

24

Forswearing it otherwise, they starch their minds.
Folkmoots, & blether, blether. John Cotton rakes
to the synod of Cambridge.
Down from my body my legs flow,
out from it arms wave, on it my head shakes.
Now Mistress Hutchinson rings forth a call—
should she? many creep out at a broken wall—
affirming the Holy Ghost
dwells in one justified. Factioning passion blinds

all to all her good, all—can she be exiled?
Bitter sister, victim! I miss you.
—I miss you, Anne,
day or night weak as a child,
tender & empty, doomed, quick to no tryst.
—I hear you. Be kind, you who leaguer
my image in the mist.
—Be kind you, to one unchained eager far & wild

and if, O my love, my heart is breaking, please
neglect my cries and I will spare you. Deep
in Time's grave, Love's, you lie still.
Lie still.—Now? That happy shape
my forehead had under my most long, rare,
ravendark, hidden, soft bodiless hair
you award me still.
You must not love me, but   I do not bid you cease.

Veiled my eyes, attending. How can it be I?
Moist, with parted lips, I listen, wicked.
I shake in the morning & retch.
Brood I do on myself naked.
A fading world I dust, with fingers new.
—I have earned the right to be alone with you.
—What right can that be?
Convulsing, if you love, enough, like a sweet lie.

Not that, I know, you can. This cratered skin,
like the crabs & shells of my Palissy ewer, touch!
Oh, you do, you do?
Falls on me what I like a witch,
for lawless holds, annihilations of law
which Time and he and man abhor, foresaw:
sharper than what my Friend
brought me for my revolt when I moved smooth & thin,

faintings black, rigour, chilling, brown
parching, back, brain burning, the grey pocks
itch, a manic stench
of pustules snapping, pain floods the palm,
sleepless, or a red shaft with a dreadful start
rides at the chapel, like a slipping heart.
My soul strains in one qualm
ah but *this* is not to save me but to throw me down.

And out of this I lull. It lessens. Kiss me.
That once. As sings out up in sparkling dark
a trail of a star & dies,
while the breath flutters, sounding, mark,
so shorn ought such caresses to us be
who, deserving nothing, flush and flee
the darkness of that light,
a lurching frozen from a warm dream. Talk to me.

—It is Spring's New England. Pussy willows wedge
up in the wet. Milky crestings, fringed
yellow, in heaven, eyed
by the melting hand-in-hand or mere
desirers single, heavy-footed, rapt,
make surge poor human hearts. Venus is trapt—
the hefty pike shifts, sheer—
in Orion blazing. Warblings, odours, nudge to an
    edge—

—Ravishing, ha, what crouches outside ought,
flamboyant, ill, angelic. Often, now,
I am afraid of you.
I am a sobersides; I know.
I *want* to take you for my lover.—Do.
—I hear a madness. Harmless I to you
am not, not I?—No.
—I cannot but be. Sing a concord of our thought.

—Wan dolls in indigo on gold: refrain
my western lust. I am drowning in this past.
I lose sight of you
who mistress me from air. Unbraced
in delirium of the grand depths, giving away
haunters what kept me, I breathe solid spray.
—I am losing you!
Straiten me on.—I suffered living like a stain:

I trundle the bodies, on the iron bars,
over that fire backward & forth; they burn;
bits fall. I wonder if
I killed them. Women serve my turn.
—Dreams! You are good.—No.—Dense with hardihood
the wicked are dislodged, and lodged the good.
In green space we are safe.
God awaits us (but I   am yielding) who Hell wars.

35

—I cannot feel myself God waits. He flies
nearer a kindly world; or he is flown.
One Saturday's rescue
won't show. Man is entirely alone
may be. I am a man of griefs & fits
trying to be my friend. And the brown smock splits,
down the pale flesh a gash
broadens and Time holds up your heart against my eyes.

—Hard and divided heaven! creases me. Shame
is failing. My breath is scented, and I throw
hostile glances towards God.
Crumpling plunge of a pestle, bray:
sin cross & opposite, wherein I survive
nightmares of Eden. Reaches foul & live
he for me, this soul
to crunch, a minute tangle of eternal flame.

I fear Hell's hammer-wind. But fear does wane.
Death's blossoms grain my hair; I cannot live.
A black joy clashes
joy, in twilight. The Devil said
'I will deal toward her softly, and her enchanting cries
will fool the horns of Adam.' Father of lies,
a male great pestle smashes
small women swarming towards the mortar's rim in vain.

38

I see the cruel spread Wings black with saints!
Silky my breasts not his, mine, mine to withhold
or tender, tender.
I am sifting, nervous, and bold.
The light is changing. Surrender this loveliness
you cannot make me do. *But* I will. Yes.
What horror, down stormy air,
warps towards me? My threatening promise faints—

torture me, Father, lest not I be thine!
Tribunal terrible & pure, my God,
mercy for him and me.
Faces half-fanged, Christ drives abroad,
and though the crop hopes, Jane is so slipshod
I cry. Evil dissolves, & love, like foam;
that love. Prattle of children powers me home,
my heart claps like the swan's
under a frenzy of *who* love me & who shine.

40

As a canoe slides by on one strong stroke
hope his hélp not I, who do hardly bear
his gift still. But whisper
I am not utterly. I pare
an apple for my pipsqueak Mercy and
she runs & all need naked apples, fanned
their tinier envies.
Vomitings, trots, rashes. Can be hope a cloak?

for the man with cropt ears glares. My fingers tighten
my skirt. I pass. Alas! I pity all.
Shy, shy, with mé, Dorothy.
Moonrise, and frightening hoots. 'Mother,
how *long* will I be dead?' Our friend the owl
vanishes, darling, but your homing soul
retires on Heaven, Mercy:
not we one instant die, only our dark does lighten.

When by me in the dusk my child sits down
I am myself. Simon, if it's that loose,
let me wiggle it out.
You'll get a bigger one there, & bite.
How they loft, how their sizes delight and grate.
The proportioned, spiritless poems accumulate.
And they publish them
away in brutish London, for a hollow crown.

Father is not himself. He keeps his bed,
and threw a saffron scum Thursday. God-forsaken
  words
escaped him raving. Save,
Lord, thy servant zealous & just.
Sam he saw back from Harvard. He did scold
his secting enemies. His stomach is cold
while we drip, while
my baby John breaks out. O far from where he bred!

Bone of moaning: sung Where he has gone
a thousand summers by truth-hallowed souls;
be still. Agh, he is gone!
Where? I know. Beyond the shoal.
Still-all a Christian daughter grinds her teeth
a little. This our land has ghosted with
our dead: I am at home.
Finish, Lord, in me this work thou hast begun.

And they tower, whom the pear-tree lured
to let them fall, fierce mornings they reclined
down the brook-bank to the east
fishing for shiners with a crookt pin,
wading, dams massing, well, and Sam's to be
a doctor in Boston. After the divisive sea,
and death's first feast,
and the galled effort on the wilderness endured,

Arminians, and the King bore against us;
of an 'inward light' we hear with horror.
Whose fan is in his hand
and he will throughly purge his floor,
come towards mé. I have what licks the joints
and bites the heart, which winter more appoints.
Iller I, oftener.
Hard at the outset; in the ending thus hard, thus?

Sacred & unutterable Mind
flashing thorough the universe one thought,
I do wait without peace.
In the article of death I budge.
Eat my sore breath, Black Angel. Let me die.
Body a-drain, when will you be dry
and countenance my speed
to Heaven's springs? lest stricter writhings have me
    declined.

'What are those pictures in the air at night,
Mother?' Mercy did ask. Space charged with faces
day & night! I place
a goatskin's fetor, and sweat: fold me
in savoury arms. Something is shaking, wrong.
He smells the musket and lifts it. It is long.
It points at my heart.
Missed he must have. In the gross storm of sunlight

I sniff a fire burning without outlet,
consuming acrid its own smoke. It's me.
Ruined laughter sounds
outside. Ah but I waken, free.
And so I am about again. I hagged
a fury at the short maid, whom tongues tagged,
and I am sorry. Once
less I was anxious when more passioned to upset

the mansion & the garden & the beauty of God.
Insectile unreflective busyness
blunts & does amend.
Hangnails, piles, fibs, life's also.
But we are that from which draws back a thumb.
The seasons stream and, somehow, I am become
an old woman. It's so:
I look. I bear to look. Strokes once more his rod.

My window gives on the graves, in our great new house
(how many burned?) upstairs, among the elms.
I lie, & endure, & wonder.
A haze slips sometimes over my dreams
and holiness on horses' bells shall stand.
Wandering pacemaker, unsteadying friend,
in a redskin calm I wait:
beat when you will our end. Sinkings & droopings
     drowse.

They say thro' the fading winter Dorothy fails,
my second, who than I bore one more, nine;
and I see her inearthed. I linger.
Seaborn she wed knelt before Simon;
Simon I, and linger. Black-yellow seething, vast
it lies fróm me, mine: all they look aghast.
It will be a glorious arm.
Docile I watch. My wreckt chest hurts when Simon
    pales.

In the yellowing days your faces wholly fail,
at Fall's onset. Solemn voices fade.
I feel no coverlet.
Light notes leap, a beckon, swaying
the tilted, sickening ear within. I'll—I'll—
I am closed & coming. Somewhere! I defile
wide as a cloud, in a cloud,
unfit, desirous, glad—even the singings veil—

—You are not ready? You áre ready. Pass,
as shadow gathers shadow in the welling night.
Fireflies of childhood torch
you down. We commit our sister down.
One candle mourn by, which a lover gave,
the use's edge and order of her grave.
Quiet? Moisture shoots.
Hungry throngs collect. They sword into the carcass.

Headstones stagger under great draughts of time
after heads pass out, and their world must reel
speechless, blind in the end
about its chilling star: thrift tuft,
whin cushion—nothing. Already with the wounded
    flying
dark air fills, I am a closet of secrets dying,
races murder, foxholes hold men,
reactor piles wage slow upon the wet brain rime.

I must pretend to leave you. Only you draw off
a benevolent phantom. I say you seem to me
drowned towns off England,
featureless as those myriads
who what bequeathed save fire-ash, fossils, burled
in the open river-drifts of the Old World?
Simon lived on for years.
I renounce not even ragged glances, small teeth,
    nothing,

O all your ages at the mercy of my loves
together lie at once, forever or
so long as I happen.
In the rain of pain & departure, still
Love has no body and presides the sun,
and elfs from silence melody. I run.
Hover, utter, still,
a sourcing   whom my lost candle like the firefly loves.

Notes

Stanzas 1–4	The poem is about the woman but this exordium is spoken by the poet, his voice modulating in stanza 4, line 8 [4.8] into hers.
1.1	He was not Governor until after her death.
1.5	Sylvester (the translator of Du Bartas) and Quarles, her favourite poets; unfortunately.
5.4, 5	Many details are from quotations in Helen Campbell's biography, the Winthrop papers, narratives, town histories.
8.4ff.	Scriptural passages are sometimes ones she used herself, as this in her *Meditation liii*.
11.8	*that one:* the Old One.
12.5–13.2	The poet interrupts.
18.8	Her first child was not born until about 1633.
22.6	*chopping:* disputing, snapping, haggling; axing.
23.1	*fere:* his friend Death.
24.1	Her irony of 22.8 intensifies.
24.2	*rakes:* inclines, as a mast; bows.
25.3	One might say: He is enabled to speak, at last, in the fortune of an echo of her—and when she is loneliest (her former spiritual adviser having deserted Anne Hutchinson, and this her closest friend banished), as if she had summoned him; and only thus, perhaps, is she enabled to hear him. This second section of the poem is a dialogue, his voice however ceasing well before it ends at 39.4, and hers continuing for the whole third part, until the coda (54–57).

29.1–4   Cf. Isa. 1:5.

29.5, 6   After a Klee.

33.1   Cf., on Byzantine icons, Frederick Rolfe ("Baron Corvo"): 'Who ever dreams of praying (with expectation of response) for the prayer of a Tintoretto or a Titian, or a Bellini, or a Botticelli? But who can refrain from crying "O Mother!" to these unruffleable wan dolls in indigo on gold?' (quoted from *The Desire and Pursuit of the Whole* by Graham Greene in *The Lost Childhood*).

33.5, 6   'Délires des grandes profondeurs,' described by Cousteau and others; a euphoria, sometimes fatal, in which the hallucinated diver offers passing fish his line, helmet, anything.

35.3, 4   As of cliffhangers, movie serials wherein each week's episode ends with a train bearing down on the strapped heroine or with the hero dangling over an abyss into which Indians above him peer with satisfaction before they hatchet the rope.

          rescue: forcible recovery (by the owner) of goods distrained.

37.7, 8   After an engraving somewhere in Fuchs's collections. *Bray*, above (36.4), puns.

39.5   The stanza is unsettled, like 24, by a middle line, signaling a broad transition.

42.8   *brutish:* her epithet for London in a kindly passage about the Great Fire.

46.1, 2   Arminians, rebels against the doctrine of unconditional election. Her husband alone opposed the law condemning Quakers to death.

46.3, 4   Matthew 3:12.

46.5, 6	Rheumatic fever, after a celebrated French description.
48.2ff.	*Space . . . outside:* delirium.
51.5	Cf. Zech. 14:20.
51.6	*Wandering pacemaker:* a disease of the heart, here the heart itself.
52.4	Seaborn Cotton, John's eldest son; Bradstreet being then magistrate.
52.5, 6	Dropsical, a complication of the last three years. Line 7 she actually said.
55.4	*thrift:* the plant, also called Our Lady's cushion.
55.8	*wet brain:* edema.
56.5, 6	Cf. G. R. Levy, *The Gate of Horn*, p. 5.

He made, a thousand years ago, a-many songs
for an Excellent lady, wif whom he was in wuv,
shall now he publish them?
Has he the right, upon that old young man,
to bare his nervous system
& display all the clouds again as they were above?

As a friend of the Court I would say, let them die.
What does anything matter? Burn them up,
put them in a bank vault.
I thought of that and when I returned to this country
I took them out again. The original fault
will not be undone by fire.

The original fault was whether wickedness
was soluble in art. History says it is,
Jacques Maritain says it is,
barely. So free them to the winds that play,
let boys & girls with these old songs have holiday
if they feel like it.

I wished, all the mild days of middle March
This special year, your blond good-nature might
(Lady) admit—kicking abruptly tight
With will and affection down your breast like starch—
Me to your story, in Spring, and stretch, and arch.
But who not flanks the wells of uncanny light
Sudden in bright sand towering? A bone sunned white.
Considering travellers bypass these and parch.

This came to less yes than an ice cream cone
Let stand . . though still my sense of it is brisk:
Blond silky cream, sweet cold, aches: a door shut.
Errors of order! Luck lies with the bone,
Who rushed (and rests) to meet your small mouth, risk
Your teeth irregular and passionate.

Who for those ages ever without some blood
Plumped for a rose and plucked it through its fence? . .
Till the canny florist, amorist of cents,
Unpawned the peppery apple, making it good
With boredom, back to its branch, as it seems he
        could,—
Vending the thornless rose. We think our rents
Paid, and we nod. O but ghosts crowd, dense,
Down in the dark shop bare stems with their Should

Not! Should Not sleepwalks where no clocks agree!
So I was not surprised, though I trembled, when
This morning groping your hand moaning your name
I heard distinctly drip . . somewhere . . and see
Coiled in our joys flicker a tongue again,
The fall of your hair a cascade of white flame.

[5]

The poet hunched, so, whom the worlds admire,
Rising as I came in; greeted me mildly,
Folded again, and our discourse was easy,
While he hid in his skin taut as a wire,
Considerate as grace, a candid pyre
Flaring some midday shore; he took more tea,
I lit his cigarette . . once I lit Yeats' as he
Muttered before an Athenaeum fire
The day Dylan had tried to slow me drunk
Down to the great man's club. But you laught just now
Letting me out, you bubbled 'Liar' and
Laught . . Well, but thén my breast was empty, monk
Of Yeatsian order: yesterday (truth now)
Flooding blurred Eliot's words sometimes,
        face not your face, hair not you blonde but iron.

[7]

I've found out why, that day, that suicide
From the Empire State falling on someone's car

Troubled you so; and why we quarrelled. War,
Illness, an accident, I can see (you cried)
But not this: what a bastard, not spring wide! . .
I said a man, life in his teeth, could care
Not much just whom he spat it on . . and far
Beyond my laugh we argued either side.

'One has a right not to be fallen on! . .'
(Our second meeting . . yellow you were wearing.)
Voices of our resistance and desire!
Did I divine then I must shortly run
Crazy with need to fall on you, despairing?
Did you bolt so, before it caught, our fire?

[9]
Great citadels whereon the gold sun falls
Miss you O Lise sequestered to the West
Which wears you Mayday lily at its breast,
Part and not part, proper to balls and brawls,
Plains, cities, or the yellow shore, not false
Anywhere, free, native and Danishest
Profane and elegant flower,—whom suggest
Frail and not frail, blond rocks and madrigals.

Once in the car (cave of our radical love)
Your darker hair I saw than golden hair
Above your thighs whiter than white-gold hair,
And where the dashboard lit faintly your least
Enlarged scene, O the midnight bloomed . . the East
Less gorgeous, wearing you like a long white glove!

10

You in your stone home where the sycamore
More than I see you sees you, where luck's grass
Smoothes your bare feet more often, even your glass
Touches your hand and tips to your lips to pour
Whatever is in it into you, through which door
O moving softness do you just now pass—
Your slippers' prows curled, red and old—alas
With what soft thought for me, at sea, and sore?

Stone of our situation, iron and stone,
Younger as days to years than the house, yet might
Wé stare as little haggard with time's roil . .
Who in each other's arms have lain—lie—one
Bite like an animal, both do, pause, and bite,
Shudder with joy, kiss . . the broad waters boil!

11

I expect you from the North. The path winds in
Between the honeysuckle and the pines, among
Poison ivy and small flowerless shrubs,
Across the red-brown needle-bed. I sit
Or smoking pace. A moment since, at six,
Mist wrapped the knoll, but now birds like a gong
Beat, greet the white-gold level shine. Wide-flung
On a thousand greens the late slight rain is gleaming.

A rabbit jumps a shrub. O my quick darling,
Lie torpid so? Cars from the highway whine,

Dawn's trunks against the sun are black. I shiver.
Your hair this fresh wind would—but I am starting.
To what end does this easy and crystal light
Dream on the flat leaves, emerald, and shimmer? . .

[13]

I lift—lift you five States away your glass,
Wide of this bar you never graced, where none
Ever I know came, where what work is done
Even by these men I know not, where a brass
Police-car sign peers in, wet strange cars pass,
Soiled hangs the rag of day out over this town,
A juke-box brains air where I drink alone,
The spruce barkeep sports a toupee alas—

My glass I lift at six o'clock, my darling,
As you plotted . . Chinese couples shift in bed,
We shared today not even filthy weather,
Beasts in the hills their tigerish love are snarling,
Suddenly they clash, I blow my short ash red,
Grey eyes light! and we have our drink together.

[14]

Moths white as ghosts among these hundreds cling
Small in the porchlight . . I am one of yours,
Doomed to a German song's stale metaphors,
The breasty thimble-rigger hums my wring.

I am your ghost, this pale ridiculous thing
Walks while you slump asleep; ouija than morse
Reaches me better; wide on Denmark's moors
I loiter, and when you slide your eyes I swing.

The billiard ball slammed in the kibitzer's mouth
Doctor nor dentist could relieve him of,
Injecting, chipping . . too he clampt it harder . .

Squalor and leech of curiosity's truth
Fork me this diamond meal to gag on love,
Grinning with passion, your astonished martyr.

[18]

You, Lise, *contrite* I never thought to see,
Whom nothing fazes, no *crise* can disconcert,
Who calm cross crises all year, flouting, alert,
A reckless lady, in whom alone agree
Of bristling states your war and peace; only
Your knuckle broke with smashing objects, curt
Classic dislike, your flowing love, expert
Flat stillness on hot sand, display you wholly.

. . And can you do what you are sorry for? . .
'I'll pin you down and put a biscuit on you'
Your childhood hissed: you didn't: just this side
Idolatry, I cannot see you sor-
ry, darling, no! what other women do
And lie or weep for, flash in your white stride.

19

You sailed in sky-high, with your speech askew
But marvellous, and talked like mad for hours,
Slamming and blessing; you transported us,
I'd never heard you talk so, and I knew—
Humbler and more proud—you each time undo
My kitcat but to cram it with these powers
You bare and bury; suddenly, late then, as
Your best 'burnt offering' took me back with you.

No jest but jostles truth! . . I burn . . am led
Burning to slaughter, passion like a sieve
Disbands my circling blood the priestess slights.
—'Remorse does not suit you at all' he said,
Rightly; but what he ragged, and might forgive,
I shook for, lawless, empty, without rights.

20

Presidential flags! and the General is here,
Shops have let out, two bands are raising hell
O hell is empty and Knowlton Street is well,
The little devils shriek, an angelic tear
Falls somewhere, so (but I laugh) would mine, I fear
The Secret Service rang the rising bell
And poor Mr Eliot and the Admiral
Have come, and a damned word nobody can hear.

Two centuries here have been abused our youth:
(Your grey eyes pierce the miles to meet my eyes)

The bicentennial of an affair with truth
(In the southern noon whom do you tyrannize?)
Not turned out well: the cast girl sucks her tooth.
(Secret, let us be true time crucifies.)

[22]

If not white shorts—then in a princess gown
Where gaslights pierce the mist I'd have your age,
Young in a grey gown, blonde and royal, rage
Of handlebars at Reisenweber's, frown
Or smile to quell or rally half the town,
To polka partners mad, to flout the stage,
To pale The Lily to an average
Woman, looking up from your champagne, or down.

Myself, ascotted, still dumb as a mome
Drinking your eyes . . No Bill comes by to cadge
A Scotch in Rector's, waving his loose tongue.
I tip my skimmer to your friend who clung
Too long, blue-stocking cracked on the *Red Badge*
Stevie's becoming known for . . We drive home.

[23]

They may suppose, because I would not cloy your ear—
If ever these songs by other ears are heard—
With 'love' and 'love', I loved you not, but blurred
Lust with strange images, warm, not quite sincere,

To switch a bedroom black. O mutineer
With me against these empty captains! gird
Your scorn again above all at *this* word
Pompous and vague on the stump of his career.

Also I fox 'heart', striking a modern breast
Hollow as a drum, and 'beauty' I taboo;
I want a verse fresh as a bubble breaks,
As little false. . . Blood of my sweet unrest
Runs all the same—I am in love with you—
Trapped in my rib-cage something throes and aches!

[24]

Still it pleads and rankles: 'Why do you love *me*?'
Replies then jammed me dumb; but now I speak,
Singing why each should *not* the other seek—
The octet will be weaker—in the fishful sea.
Your friends I don't like all, and poetry
You less than music stir to, the blue streak
Troubles me you drink: if all these are weak
Objections, they are all, and all I foresee.

Your choice, though!. . Who no Goliath has slung low.
When one day rushing about your lawn you saw
Him whom I might not name without some awe
If curious Johnson should enquire below,
'Who lifts this voice harsh, fresh, and beautiful?'
—'As thy soul liveth, O king, I cannot tell.'

Sometimes the night echoes to prideless wailing
Low as I hunch home late and fever-tired,
Near you not, nearing the sharer I desired,
Toward whom till now I sailed back; but that sailing
Yaws, from the cabin orders like a failing
Dribble, the stores disordered and then fired
Skid wild, the men are glaring, the mate has wired
Hopeless: locked in, and humming, the Captain's nailing
A false log to the lurching table. Lies
And passion sing in the cabin on the voyage home,
The burgee should fly Jolly Roger: wind
Madness like the tackle of a crane (outcries
Ascend) around to heave him from the foam
Irresponsible, since all the stars rain blind.

Of all that weeks-long day, though call it back
If I will I can—rain thrice, sheets, a torrent
Spaced by the dry sun, Sunday thirst that went
Sharp-set from town to town, down cul-de-sac
To smoke a blind pig for a liquid snack,
Did ever beer taste better, when opulent
Over the State line with the State's consent
We cleared our four throats, climbing off the rack;
Lost our way then: our thirst again: then tea
With a velvet jacket over the flowered choker
Almost a man, who copied tulips *queerer*:
Dinner a triumph—of that day I have wholly

One moment (weeks I played the friendly joker)
Your eyes married to mine in the car mirror.

[31]

Troubling are masks . . the faces of friends, my face
Met unawares and your face: where I mum
Your doubleganger writhes, wraiths are we come
To keep a festival, none but wraiths embrace;
Our loyal rite only we interlace,
Laertes' winding-sheet done and undone
In Ithaca by day and night . . we thrum
Hopeful our shuffles, trusting to our disgrace.

Impostors . . O but our truth our fortunes cup
To flash this lying blood. Sore and austere
The crown we cry for, merely to lie ill
In grand evasion, questions *not come up.*—
I am dreaming on the hour when I can hear
My last lie rattle, and then lie truly still.

[33]

Audacities and fêtes of the drunken weeks!
One step false pitches all down . . come and pour
Another . . Strange, warningless we four
Locked, crocked together, two of us made sneaks—
Who can't get at each other—midnights of freaks
On crepitant surfaces, a kiss blind from the door . .

One head suspects, drooping and vaguely sore,
Something entirely sad, skew, she not seeks . .

'You'll give me ulcers if all this keeps up'
You moaned . . One only, ignorant and kind,
Saves his own life useful and usual,
Blind to the witch-antinomy I sup
Spinning between the laws on the black edge, blind
Head—O do I?—I dance to disannul.

[36]

Keep your eyes open when you kiss: do: when
You kiss. All silly time else, close them to;
Unsleeping, I implore you (dear) pursue
In darkness me, as I do you again
Instantly we part . . only me both then
And when your fingers fall, let there be two
Only, 'in that dream-kingdom': I would have you
Me alone recognize your citizen.

Before who wanted eyes, making love, so?
I do now. However we are driven and hide,
What state we keep all other states condemn,
We see ourselves, we watch the solemn glow
Of empty courts we kiss in . . Open wide!
You do, you do, and I look into them.

Sigh as it ends . . I keep an eye on your
Amour with Scotch,—too *cher* to consummate;
Faster your disappearing beer than late-
ly mine; your naked passion for the floor;
Your hollow leg; your hanker for one more
Dark as the Sundam Trench; how you dilate
Upon psychotics of this class, collate
Stages, and . . how long since you, well, *forbore*.

Ah, but the high fire sings on to be fed
Whipping our darkness by the lifting sea
A while, O darling drinking like a clock.
The tide comes on: spare, Time, from what you spread
Her story,—tilting a frozen Daiquiri,
Blonde, barefoot, beautiful,
    flat on the bare floor rivetted to Bach.

You should be gone in winter, that Nature mourn
With me your anarch separation, call-
ing warmth all with you: as more poetical
Than to be left biting the dog-days, lorn
Alone when all else burgeons, brides are born,
Children yet (some) begotten, every wall
Clasped by its vine here . . crony alcohol
Comfort as random as the unicorn.

Listen, for poets are feigned to lie, and I
For you a liar am a thousand times,
Scars of these months blazon like a decree:
I would have you—a liner pulls the sky—
Trust when I mumble me. Than gin-&-limes
You are cooler, darling, O come back to me.

[46]

Are we? You murmur 'not'. What of the night
Attack on the dark road we could not contain,
Twice I slid to you sudden as the stain
Joy bloods the wanderer at the water's sight,
And back, but you writhed on me . . as I write
I tremble . . trust me not to keep on sane
Until you whisper 'Come to me again'
Unless you whisper soon. O come we soon
Together dark and sack each other outright,
Doomed cities loose and thirsty as a dune . .
Lovers we are, whom now the on-tide licks.
Our fast of famed sleep stirs, darling, diurnal,—
Hurry! till we, beginning our eternal
Junket on the winds, wake like a ton of Styx.

[47]

How far upon these songs with my strict wrist
Hard to bear down, who knows? None is to read
But you: so gently . . but then truth's to heed,
The sole word, near or far, shot in the mist.

Double I sing, I must, your utraquist,
Crumpling a syntax at a sudden need,
Stridor of English softening to plead
O to you plainly lest you more resist.

'Arthur lay then at Caerlon upon Usk . .'
I see, and all that story swims back . . red
Satin over rushes . . Mother's voice at dusk.

So I comb times and men to cram you rare:
'Faire looketh *Ceres* with her yellow Haire'—
Fairer you far O here lie filteréd.

[51]

A tongue there is wags, down in the dark wood O:
Trust it not. It trills malice among friends,
Irrelevant squibs and lies, to its own ends
Or to no ends, simply because it would O.
To us, us most I hear, it prinks no good O;
Has its idea, Jamesian; apprehends
Truth non-aviarian; meddles, and 'defends'
Honour free . . that such a bill so wily should O!

Who to my hand all year flew to be fed
Makes up his doubts to dart at us . . Ah well,
Did you see the *green* of that catalpa tree?—
A certain jackal will lose half its head
For cheek, our keek, our hairy philomel.—
How can you tell?—A little bird told me.

It was the sky all day I grew to and saw.
I cycled southeast through the empty towns,
Flags hanging out, between the summer grains,
Meeting mainly the azure minions of our law.

Near our fake lake an artificial pool
Was full of men and women; all the rest,
Shore for the Fourth. I crookt two roses. Most
I studied the sky's involuntary rule.

I followed a cloud and finally I caught it,
Springing my ribbon down the world of green . .
Shadow to shadow, under tropical day . .

Flat country, slow, alone. So in my pocket
Your snapshot nightmares where (cloth, flesh between)
My heart was, before I gave it away.

Today is it? Is it today? I shudder
For nothing in my chair, and suddenly yawn.
Today I suddenly believe. Since dawn
When I got up, my muscles like a rudder
Strain crosswise from this work. I rise and mutter
Something, and hum, pace, and sit down again
Hard. A butterfly in my shoulder then
Stops and aches. My stomach swings like a shutter.

As the undergrounds piston a force of air
Before their crash into the station, you
Are felt before your coming, and the platforms shake.
So light, so small, so far still, to impair
Action and peace so . . risks we take make true
Maybe our safeties . . *come* for our risk's sake.

Astronomies and slangs to find you, dear,
Star, art-breath, crowner, conscience! and to chart
For kids unborn your distal beauty, part
On part that startles, till you blaze more clear
And witching than your sister Venus here
To a late age can, though her senior start
Is my new insomnia,—swift sleepless art
To draw you even . . and to draw you near.

I prod our English: cough me up a word,
Slip me an epithet will justify
My daring fondle, fumble of far fire
Crackling nearby, unreasonable as a surd,
A flash of light, an insight: I am the shy
Vehicle of your cadmium shine . . your choir.

Faith like the warrior ant swarming, enslaving
Or griding others, you gave me soft as dew,

My darling, drawing me suddenly into you,
Your arms' strong kindness at my back, your weaving
Thighs agile to me, white teeth in your heaving
Hard, your face bright and dark, back, as we screw
Our lives together—twin convulsion—blue
Crests curl, to rest . . again the ivy waving.

Faiths other fall. Afterwards I kissed you
So (Lise) long, and your eyes so waxed, marine,
Wider I drowned . . light to their surface drawn
Down met the wild light (derelict weeks I missed you
Leave me forever) upstreaming; never-seen,
Your radiant glad soul surfaced in the dawn.

[68]

Where the lane from the highway swerves the first
    drops fell
Like lead, I bowed my head and drifted up.
Now in the grove they pat like footsteps, but
Not hers, Despair's. In slant lines sentinel
Silver and thin, it rains so into Hell,
Unvisited these thousand years. I grope
A little in the wind after a hope
For sun before she wakes . . all might be well.

All might yet be well . . I wandered just
Down to the upper lane now, the sky was clearing,
And as I scrawl, the sun breaks. Ah, what use?
She said if rain, *no*,—in vain self-abuse

I lie a fairy well! cloud disappearing
Not lonelier, leaving like me: we must.

[70]

Under Scorpion both, back in the Sooner State
Where the dry winds winnow the soul, we both were
      born,
And we have cast our origin, and the Horn
Neither has frankly scanted, others imitate
Us; and we have come a long way, late
For depth enough, betimes enough for torn
Hangnails of nerves and innocent love, we turn
Together in this vize lips, eyes, our Fate.

When the cam slid, the prodigious fingers tightened
And we began to fuse, weird afternoon
Early in May (the Third), we both were frightened;
A month we writhed, in sudden love like a scrimmage;
June's wide loss worse; the fortnight after June
Worst. Vize and woe worked us this perfect image!

[71]

Our Sunday morning when dawn-priests were applying
Wafer and wine to the human wound, we laid
Ourselves to cure ourselves down: I'm afraid
Our vestments wanted, but Francis' friends were crying
In the nave of pines, sun-satisfied, and flying

Subtle as angels about the barricade
Boughs made over us, deep in a bed half made
Needle-soft, half the sea of our simultaneous dying.

'Death is the mother of beauty.' Awry no leaf
Shivering with delight, we die to be well . .
Careless with sleepy love, so long unloving.
What if our convalescence must be brief
As we are, the matin meet the passing bell? . .
About our pines our sister, wind, is moving.

[72]

A Cambridge friend put in,—one whom I used
To pay small rope at chess to, who in vain
Luffed up to free a rook,—and through the strain
Of ten-year-old talk cocktails partly loosed
I forgot you, forgot you, for the first
Hour in months of watches . . Mozart's pain
I heard then, in the cranny of the hurricane,
As since the chrisom caught me up immersed

I have heard nothing but the sough of the sea
And wide upon the open sea my friend
The sea-wind crying, out of its cave to roam
No more, no more . . until my memory
Swung you back like a lock: I sing the end,
Tolerant Aeolus to call me home.

Demand me again what Kafka's riddles mean,
For I am the penal colony's prime scribe:
From solitary, firing against the tribe
Uncanny judgments ancient and unclean.
I am the officer flat on my own machine,
Priest of the one Law no despair can bribe,
On whom the mort-prongs hover to inscribe
'I FELL IN LOVE' . . O none of this foreseen,
Adulteries and divorces cold I judged
And strapped the tramps flat. Now the harrow trembles
Down, a strap snaps, I wave—out of control—
To you to change the legend has not budged
These years: make the machine grave on me (stumbles
Someone to latch the strap) 'I MET MY SOUL'.

Fall and rise of her midriff bells. I watch.
Blue knee-long shorts, striped light shirt. Bright
    between
Copt hills of the cushion a lazy green
Her sun-incomparable face I watch.
A darkness dreams adown her softest crotch,
A hand dreams on her breast, two fingers lean,
The ring shows like a wound. Her hair swirls clean
Alone in the vague room's morning-after botch.

Endymion's Glaucus through a thousand years
Collected the bodies of lovers lost, until

His own beloved's body rustled and sighed . .
So I would, O to spring—blotting her fears,
The others in this house, the house, road, hill—
As once she up the stair sprang to me, lips wide!

[78]

On the wheat-sacks, sullen with the ceaseless damp,
William and I sat hours and talked of you,
I talked of you. Potting porter. Just a few
Fireflies were out, no stars, no moon; no lamp.
The Great Dane licked my forearm like a stamp,
Surprisingly, in total darkness. Who
Responds with peaceful gestures, calm and new
This while, your home-strong love's ferocious tramp?

Insonorous and easy night! I lusk,
Until we rise and strike rake-handles in
The nervous sacks to prod and mix with air;
Lest a flame sing out invisible and brusk
About the black barn . . Kingston (and my chin
Sank on the rake-end) suddenly
      I longed for sick, your toxic music there.

[79]

I dreamt he drove me back to the asylum
Straight after lunch; we stood then at one end,
A sort of cafeteria behind, my friend

Behind me, nuts in groups about the room;
A dumbwaiter with five shelves was waiting (some-
thing's missing here) to take me up—I bend
And lift a quart of milk to hide and tend,
Take with me. Everybody is watching, dumb.

I try to put it first among some worm-
shot volumes of the N.E.D. I had
On the top shelf—then somewhere else . . slowly
Lise comes up in a matron's uniform
And with a look (I saw once) infinitely sad
In her grey eyes takes it away from me.

[82]

Why can't, Lise, why shouldn't *they* fall in love?
Mild both, both still in mix of studies, still
Unsteadied into life, novices of the will,
Formed upon others (us), disciples of
The Master and the revisionists: enough
Apart from their attraction, to unstill
The old calm loves (cyclonic loves) until
The electric air shocks them together, rough,
But better in love than grief, who can afford
No storms (ours). Fantasy! . . . Forget.
—I write this leaving Pennsylvania's farms,
Seats 37, 12 Standees, I am tired
Unspeakably of standing: Kiss me, and let
Let me sit down and take you in my arms.

Our lives before bitterly our mistake!—
We should have been together seething years,
We should have been the tomb-bat hangs and hears
Sounds inconceivable, been a new snowflake,
We should have been the senile world's one sake,
Vestigial lovers, tropical and fierce
Among fatigues and snows, the gangs and queers,
We should have been the bloom of a cockcrow lake.

. . A child's moon, child's fire!—What I love of you
Inter alia tingles like a whole good day,
A hard wind, or a Strad's consummate pluck,
Proficient, full and strong, shrewd as the blue
Profound sky, pale as a winter sky you lay
And with these breasts whiter than stars gave suck.

Anomalous I linger, and ignore
My blue conviction she will now not come
Whose grey eyes blur before me like some sum
A shifting riddle to fatigue . . I pore . .
Faster they flicker, and flag, moving on slower,
And I move with them—who am I? a scum
Thickens on a victim, a delirium
Begins to mutter, which I must explore.

O rapt as Monteverdi's '. . *note* . . *note* . .'
I glide aroused—a rumour? or a dream?

An actual lover? Elmo's light? erlking?
—'I know very well who I am' said Don Quixote.
The sourceless lightning laps my stare, the stream
Backs through the wood, the cosy spiders cling.

[94]

Most strange, my change, this nervous interim.—
The utter courtship ended, tokens won,
Assurance salted down . . all this to stun
More than excite: I blink about me grim
And dull and anxious, rather than I skim
Light bright & confident: like a weak pun
I stumble neither way: Hope weighs a ton:
Tired certainly, but much less tired than dim.

—I were absence' adept, a glaring eye;
Or I were agile to this joy, this letter,
You say from Fox Hill: '*I am not the same.*'—
No more am I: I'm neither: without you I
Am not myself. My sight is dying. Better
The searchlights' torture which we overcame!

[96]

It will seem strange, no more this range on range
Of opening hopes and happenings. Strange to be
One's *name* no longer. Not caught up, not free.
Strange, not to wish one's wishes onward. Strange,

The looseness, slopping, time and space estrange.
Strangest, and sad as a blind child, not to see
Ever you, never to hear you, endlessly
Neither you there, nor coming . . Heavy change!—

An instant there is, Sophoclean, true,
When Oedipus must understand: his head—
When Oedipus *believes!*—tilts like a wave,
And will not break, only ἰού ἰού
Wells from his dreadful mouth, the love he led:
Prolong to Procyon this. This begins my grave.

[97]

I say *I laid siege—you enchanted me* . .
Magic and warfare, faithful metaphors
As when their paleolithic woods and tors
The hunter and the witchwife roamed, half free,
Half to the Provider and the Mystery-
riddler bound: the kill, the spell: your languors
I wag my wolf's tail to—without remorse?—
You shudder as I'd pierce you where I knee

l . . Only we little wished, or you to charm
Or I to make you shudder, you to wreck
Or I to hum you daring on my arm.
Abrupt as a dogfight, the air full of
Tails and teeth—the meshing of a trek—
All this began: knock-down-and-drag-out love.

I am interested alone in making ready,
Pointed, more splendid, O the Action which
Attends your whim; bridge interim; enrich
That unimaginable-still, with study
So sharp at time the probe shivers back bloody;
Test the strange circuit but to trust the switch.
The Muse is real, the random shades I stitch—
Devoted vicarage—somewhere real, and steady.

Burnt cork, my leer, my Groucho crouch and rush,
No more my nature than Cyrano's: we
Are 'hindered characters' and mock the time,
The curving and incomprehensible hush
Einstein requires before that colloquy
Altared of joy concludes our pantomime!

Because I'd seen you not believe your lover,
Because you scouted cries come from no cliff,
Because to supplications you were stiff
As Ciro, O as Nero to discover
Slow how your subject loved you, I would hover
Between the slave and rebel—till this life
Arrives: '. . was astonished as I would be if
I leaned against a house and the house fell over . .'

Well, it fell over, over: trust him now:
A stronger house than looked—*you leaned*, and crash,
My walls and ceiling were to be walked on.—

The same thing happened once in Chaplin, how
He solved it now I lose.—Walk on the trash . .
Walk, softly, triste,—little is really gone.

[103]

A 'broken heart' . . but *can* a heart break, now?
Lovers have stood bareheaded in love's 'storm'
Three thousand years, changed by their mistress'
    'charm',
Fitted their 'torment' to a passive bow,
Suffered the 'darts' under a knitted brow,
And has one heart *broken* for all this 'harm'?
An arm is something definite. My arm
Is acting—I hardly know to tell you how.

It aches . . well, after fifteen minutes of
Serving, I can't serve more, it's not my arm,
A piece of pain joined to me, helpless dumb thing.
After four months of work-destroying love
(An hour, I still don't lift it: I feel real alarm:
Weeks of this,—no doctor finds a thing),
    not much; and not all. Still, this is something.

[104]

A spot of poontang on a five-foot piece,
Diminutive, but room *enough* . . like clay
To finger eager on some torrid day . .

Who'd throw her black hair back, and hang, and tease.
Never, not once in all one's horny lease
To have had a demi-lay, a pretty, gay,
Snug, slim and supple-breasted girl for play . .
She bats her big, warm eyes, and slides like grease.

And cuff her silly-hot again, mouth hot
And wet her small round writhing—but this screams
Suddenly awake, unreal as alkahest,
My God, this isn't what I *want!*—You tot
The harrow-days you hold me to, black dreams,
The dirty water to get off my chest.

[106]

Began with swirling, blind, unstilled oh still,—
The tide had set in toward the western door
And I was working with the tide, I bore
My panful of reflexion firm, until
A voice arrested me,—body, and will,
And panful, wheeled and split, tempted nerves tore,
And all uncome time blackened like the core
Of an apple on through man's heart moving still . .

At nine o'clock and thirty Thursday night,
In Nineteen XXXX, February
Twice-ten-day, by a doorway in McIntosh,
So quietly neither the rip's cold slosh
Nor the meshing of great wheels warned me, unwary,
An enigmatic girl smiled out my sight.

Darling I wait O in my upstairs box
O for your footfall, O for your footfáll
in the extreme heat—I don't mind at all,
it's silence has me and the no of clocks
keeping us isolated longer: rocks
did the first martyr and will do to stall
our enemies, I'll get up on the roof of the hall
and heave freely. The University of Soft Knocks

will headlines in the *Times* make: Fellow goes mad,
crowd panics, rhododendrons injured. Slow
will flow the obituaries while the facts get straight,
almost straight. He was in love and he was had.
That was it: he should have stuck to his own mate,
before he went a-coming across the sea-O.

I owe you, do I not, a roofer: though
My sister-*in*-law and her nephews stayed,
Not I stayed. O kind sister-outlaw, laid
Far off and legally four weeks, stoop low,
For my true thanks are fugitive also
Only to you;—stop off your cant, you jade,
Bend down,—*I* have not ever disobeyed
You; and you will hear what it is I owe.

I owe you thanks for evenings in that house
When . . neither here, nor there, no where, were you,

Nights like long knives; . . *two* letters! . . times when
       your voice
Nearly I latched. Another debit to
Your kinder husband. From the country of Choice
Another province chopt,—and they were few.

[109]

Ménage à trois, like Tristan's,—difficult! . .
The convalescent Count; his mistress; fast
The wiry wild arthritic young fantast
In love with her, his genius occult,
His weakness blazing, ugly, an insult
A salutation; in his yacht they assed
Up and down the whole coast six months . . last
It couldn't: . . the pair to Paris. Chaos, result.

Well—but four worse!! . . all four, marvellous friends—
Some horse-shit here, eh?—You admitted it,
Come, you did once . . and we *are friends*, I say.—
'La Cuchiani aima Tristan, mais . .'
(The biographer says) *unscrupulous* a bit,
Or utterly . . . There, of course, the resemblance ends.

[112]

I break my pace now for a sonic boom,
the future's with & in us. I sit fired
but comes on strong with the fire fatigue: I'm tired.

'I'd drive my car across the living-room
if I could get it inside the house.' You loom
less, less than before when your voice choired
into my transept hear I now it, not expired
but half-dead with exhaustion, like Mr Bloom.

Dazzle, before I abandon you, my eyes,
my eyes which I need for journeys difficult
in which case it may be said that I survive you.
Your voice continues, with its lows & highs,
and I am a willing accomplice in the cult
and every word that I   have gasped of you is true.

'I didn't see anyone else, I just saw Lise'
Anne Frank remorseful from the grave: ah well,
it was a vision of her mother in Hell,
a payment beforehand for rebellion's seize,
whereby she grew up: springing from her knees
she saw her parents level. I ward your spell
away, and I try hard to look at you level
but that is quite unaccustomed to me, Lise.

Months I lookt up, entranced by you up there
like a Goya ceiling which will not come down,
in swirling clouds, until the end is here.
Tetélestai. We steamed in a freighter from Spain
& I will never see those frescoes again
nor need to, having memorized your cloudy gown.

You come blonde visiting through the black air
knocking on my hinged lawn-level window
and you will come for years, above, below,
& through to interrupt my study where
I'm sweating it out like asterisks: so there,—
you are the text, my work's broken down so
I found, after my grandmother died, slow,
and I had flown far South to her funeral spare

but crowded with relations, I found her last
letter unopened, much less answered: shame
overcame me so far I paused & cried
in my underground study, for all the past
undone & never again to walk tall, lame
at the mercy of your presence to abide.

All we were going strong last night this time,
the *mots* were flying & the frozen daiquiris
were downing, supine on the floor lay Lise
listening to Schubert grievous & sublime,
my head was frantic with a following rime:
it was a good evening, an evening to please,
I kissed her in the kitchen—ecstasies—
among so much good we tamped down the crime.

The weather's changing. This morning was cold,
as I made for the grove, without expectation,

some hundred Sonnets in my pocket, old,
to read her if she came. Presently the sun
yellowed the pines & my lady came not
in blue jeans & a sweater. I sat down & wrote.

HIS THOUGHT MADE POCKETS & THE PLANE BUCKT | 1958

Henry sats in de plane & was gay.
Careful Henry nothing said aloud
but where a virgin out of cloud
to her Mountain dropt in light
his thought made pockets & the plane buckt.
'Parm me, Lady.' 'Orright.'

The Poet's Final Instructions

Dog-tired, suisired, will now my body down
near Cedar Avenue in Minneap,
when my crime comes. I am blazing with hope.
Do me glory, come the whole way across town.

I couldn't rest from hell just anywhere,
in commonplaces. Choiring & strange my pall!
I might not lie still in the waste of St Paul
or buy DAD'S root beer; good signs I forgive.

Drop here, with honour due, my trunk & brain
among the passioning of my countrymen
unable to read, rich, proud of their tags
and proud of me. Assemble all my bags!
Bury me in a hole, and give a cheer,
near Cedar on Lake Street, where the used cars live.

FROM **The Black Book (i)**

Grandfather, sleepless in a room upstairs,
Seldom came down; so when they tript him down
We wept. The blind light sang about his ears,
Later we heard. Brother had pull. In pairs
He, some, slept upon stone.
Later they stamped him down in mud.
The windlass drew him silly & odd-eyed, blood
Broke from his ears before they quit.
Before they trucked him home they cleaned him up
      somewhat.

Only the loose eyes' glaze they could not clean
And soon he died. He howled a night and shook
Our teeth before the end; we breathed again
When he stopt. Abraham, what we have seen
Write, I beg, in your Book.
No more the solemn and high bells
Call to our pall; we call or gibber; Hell's
Irritable & treacherous
Despairs here here (not him) reach now to shatter us.

FROM **The Black Book (iii)**

Lover & child, a little sing.
From long-lockt cattle-cars who grope
Who near a place of showers come
Foul no more, whose murmuring

Grows in a hiss of gas will clear them home:
Away from & toward me: a little soap,
Disrobing, *Achtung!* in a dirty hope,
They shuffle with their haircuts in to die.
Lift them an elegy, poor you and I,
Fair & strengthless as seafoam
Under a deserted sky.

A Sympathy, A Welcome

Feel for your bad fall how could I fail,
poor Paul, who had it so good.
I can offer you only: this world like a knife.
Yet you'll get to know your mother
and humourless as you do look you will laugh
and all the others
will NOT be fierce to you, and loverhood
will swing your soul like a broken bell
deep in a forsaken wood, poor Paul,
whose wild bad father loves you well.

Note to Wang Wei

How could you be so happy, now some thousand years
disheveled, puffs of dust?
It leaves me uneasy at last,
your poems teaze me to the verge of tears
and your fate. It makes me think.
It makes me long for mountains & blue waters.
Makes me wonder how much to allow.
(I'm reconfirming, God of bolts & bangs,
of fugues & bucks, whose rocket burns & sings.)
I wish we could meet for a drink
in a 'freedom from ten thousand matters.'
Be dust myself pretty soon; not now.

The Will

A frail vague man, in whom our senses ached
With nothing, began to whisper with himself
At line-up, from the rear,—
We trembled for him,—shook the scald that caked
His skull, totting up phantoms none could solve,
Fag-end of a career.
(Shadowless in a cairn, four lights. Farewell,
The legacy trots off,
A swimming moment of the stiff's desire
Such decades since. Or nothing trots to tell
Intestate once with love
Pain brain stood up a bit out of time's mire.)
He scrambled one night out
And dodged between their lights far to the wire,
Where he lodged. I suppose he crisped, dying in fire;
A shot or so, a shout;
But certainly, lifting our scalps, well beyond fear,
He suddenly sang, sang, hanging on the wire.

from The Black Book

Waiting

Nearer, my heart, to me . . . My cigarette
Endures an apotheosis; I feel
More for the grey twirl than I mull or whet
God's promise . . . probably the butt is real.

Now I seem less so. Than tissue & ash
I am more indistinct, than fire and weed
Yielding to fire, as fire to the weed's trash:
Do pins & feathers kill? Can a root bleed?

Master my heart will nothing to my side?
Otherwhere, neither broods nor aches for me
Regitive by the iron door unterrified
Foully it leans. That hole, my mystery,

Which once its bolt, the muscle of their State,
Opened to drop me in, cannot keep shut!
Lancet intensities I anticipate!
Feathery movement twires about my thought!

The frontier posts, disfigured sphincters, spill
Invaders home; heart through the ribs returns;
How corn & wine return, transfigured, fill
Sleepy lands, our land. Ice on my brow burns,

Ebbing, blackfellow-dull, when the bolt shoots
Over the tigerish flood may I soar steady
Whither the latched starless & heartless roots
O need blindly night. I am almost ready—

from The Black Book

Of Isaac Rosenfeld

I never knew him. We hailed, here or there,
and friendly words about each other's bad
& halfway works we mouthed, and clowned. I had
briefings on him, years, over the waters. Fair
showed yet his promise; he enjoyed despair,
did wrong, set living people roaring or sad,
loved was, empty months mastered, sore made & glad
a wife, and liked children—from across, not down;
and so they loved them back. Only they said
'He ought to be a father, not a child'—
his own child too said so. I have to glare
into a room where, half-through, he crampt dead,
where all his lovers, seeking his cry, drown,
and solo I reel in a word dispelled.

Formal Elegy

I

A hurdle of water, and O these waters are cold
(warm at outset) in the dirty end.
Murder on murder on murder, where I stagger,
whiten the good land where we have held out.
These kills were not for loot,
however Byzantium hovers in the mind:
were matters of principle—that's worst of all—
& fear & crazed mercy.
Ruby, with his mad claim

he shot to spare the Lady's testifying,
probably is sincere.
No doubt, in his still cell, his mind sits pure.

II

Yes, it looks like a wilderness—pacem appellant.
Honour to Patrolman Tippit. Peace to the rifler's
    widow.
Seven, I believe, play fatherless.

III

Scuppered the yachts, the choppers, big cars, jets.
Nobody goes anywhere,
lengthened (days) into TV.
I am four feet long, invisibly.
What in the end will be left of us is a stare,
underwater.
If you want me to join you in confident prayer, let's
not.
I sidled in & past, gazing upon it,
the bier.

IV

Too Andean hopes, now angry shade.—
I am an automobile. Into me climb
many, and go their ways. Onto him climbed
a-many and went his way.
For a while we seemed to be having a holiday
off from ourselves—ah, but the world is wigs,
as sudden we came to feel
and even hís splendid hair kept not wholly real

fumbling & falsing in & out of the Bay of Pigs,
the bad moment of this excellent man,
suffered by me as a small car can.
Faithful to course we stayed.

V

Some in their places are constrained to weep.
Stunned, more, though.
Black foam. A weaving snake. An invulnerable sleep.
It doing have to come so.
All at once, hurtless, in the tide of applause
& expectation. I write from New York
where except for a paraplegic exterminator—
a gracious & sweet guy—
nobody has done no work
lately

VI

It's odd perhaps that Dallas   cannot after their crimes
criminals protect or Presidents.
Fat Dallas, a fit set.
I would not perhaps have voted for him next time.
Images of Mr Kennedy blue the air,
who is little now, with no chance to grow great,
but who have set his touch across the State,
true-intended, strong

VII

My breath comes heavy, does my breath.
I feel heavy about the President's death.

VIII

I understand I hear I see I read
schoolgirls in Dallas when the white word came
or slammed, cheered in their thoughtful grades,
brought-up to a loving tone.
I do not sicken but somewhat with shame
I shift my head an inch; who are my own.
I have known a loving Texas   woman in parades
and she was boastful & treacherous.
That boringest of words, whereas here I blush,
"education," peters to a nailing of us.

IX

An editor has asked me in my name
what wish or prophecy I'd like to state
for the new year. I am silent on these occasions
steadily, having no love for a fool
(which I keep being) but I break my rule:
I do all-wish the bullets swim astray
sent to the President, and that all around
help, and his heart keep sound.
I have a strange sense
                          he's about to be the best of men.
Amen.

X

It's quiet at Arlington. Rock Creek is quiet.
My prīmers, with Mount Auburn. Everybody should
have his sweet boneyards. Yet let the young not go,
our apprentice King! Alas,
muffled, he must. He seemed good:

brainy in riot, daring, cool.
                              So
let us abandon the scene of disorder. Drop
them shattered bodies into tranquil places,
where moulder as you will. We compose our faces
cold as the cresting waters; ready again.
The waters break.
All black & white together, stunned, survive
the final insolence to the head of you;
bow.
Overwhelmed-un, live.
A rifle fact is over, pistol facts
almost entirely are too.
The man of a wise face opened it to speak:
Let us continue.

1

Huffy Henry hid   the day,
unappeasable Henry sulked.
I see his point,—a trying to put things over.
It was the thought that they thought
they could *do* it made Henry wicked & away.
But he should have come out and talked.

All the world like a woolen lover
once did seem on Henry's side.
Then came a departure.
Thereafter nothing fell out as it might or ought.
I don't see how Henry, pried
open for all the world to see, survived.

What he has now to say is a long
wonder the world can bear & be.
Once in a sycamore I was glad
all at the top, and I sang.
Hard on the land wears the strong sea
and empty grows every bed.

3

A Stimulant for an Old Beast

Acacia, burnt myrrh, velvet, pricky stings.
—I'm not so young but not so very old,
said screwed-up lovely 23.
A final sense of being right out in the cold,
unkissed.
(—My psychiatrist can lick your psychiatrist.) Women
        get under things.

All these old criminals sooner or later
have had it. I've been reading old journals.
Gottwald & Co., out of business now.
Thick chests quit. Double agent, Joe.
She holds her breath like a seal
and is whiter & smoother.

Rilke was a *jerk*.
I admit his griefs & music
& titled spelled all-disappointed ladies.
A threshold worse than the circles
where the vile settle & lurk,
Rilke's. As I said,—

4

Filling her compact & delicious body
with chicken páprika, she glanced at me
twice.

Fainting with interest, I hungered back
and only the fact of her husband & four other people
kept me from springing on her

or falling at her little feet and crying
'You are the hottest one for years of night
Henry's dazed eyes
have enjoyed, Brilliance.' I advanced upon
(despairing) my spumoni.—Sir Bones: is stuffed,
de world, wif feeding girls.

—Black hair, complexion Latin, jewelled eyes
downcast . . . The slob beside her   feasts . . . What
     wonders is
she sitting on, over there?
The restaurant buzzes. She might as well be on Mars.
Where did it all go wrong? There ought to be a law
     against Henry.
—Mr. Bones: there is.

13
God bless Henry. He lived like a rat,
with a thatch of hair on his head
in the beginning.
Henry was not a coward. Much.
He never deserted anything; instead
he stuck, when things like pity were thinning.

So may be Henry was a human being.
Let's investigate that.
. . . We did; okay.
He is a human American man.
That's true. My lass is braking.
My brass is aching. Come & diminish me, & map my
        way.

God's Henry's enemy. We're in business . . . Why,
what business must be clear.
A cornering.
I couldn't feel more like it.—Mr Bones,
as I look on the saffron sky,
you strikes me as ornery.

14

Life, friends, is boring. We must not say so.
After all, the sky flashes, the great sea yearns,
we ourselves flash and yearn,
and moreover my mother told me as a boy
(repeatingly) 'Ever to confess you're bored
means you have no

Inner Resources.' I conclude now I have no
inner resources, because I am heavy bored.
Peoples bore me,
literature bores me, especially great literature,
Henry bores me, with his plights & gripes
as bad as achilles,

who loves people and valiant art, which bores me.
And the tranquil hills, & gin, look like a drag
and somehow a dog
has taken itself & its tail considerably away
into mountains or sea or sky, leaving
behind: me, wag.

18
A Strut for Roethke

Westward, hit a low note, for a roarer lost
across the Sound but north from Bremerton,
hit a way down note.
And never cadenza again of flowers, or cost.
Him who could really do that cleared his throat
& staggered on.

The bluebells, pool-shallows, saluted his over-needs,
while the clouds growled, heh-heh, & snapped, &
　　　　crashed.

No stunt he'll ever unflinch once more will fail
(O lucky fellow, eh Bones?)—drifted off upstairs,
downstairs, somewheres.
No more daily, trying to hit the head on the nail:
thirstless: without a think in his head:
back from wherever, with it said.

Hit a high long note, for a lover found
needing a lower into friendlier ground

to bug among worms no more
around um jungles where ah blurt 'What for?'
Weeds, too, he favoured as   most men don't favour
    men.
The Garden Master's gone.

Of 1826

I am the little man who smokes & smokes.
I am the girl who does know better but.
I am the king of the pool.
I am so wise I had my mouth sewn shut.
I am a government official & a goddamned fool.
I am a lady who takes jokes.

I am the enemy of the mind.
I am the auto salesman and lóve you.
I am a teenage cancer, with a plan.
I am the blackt-out man.
I am the woman powerful as a zoo.
I am two eyes screwed to my set, whose blind—

It is the Fourth of July.
Collect: while the dying man,
forgone by you creator, who forgives,
is gasping 'Thomas Jefferson still lives'
in vain, in vain, in vain.
I am Henry Pussy-cat! My whiskers fly.

The Lay of Ike

This is the lay of Ike.
Here's to the glory of the Great White—awk—
who has been running—er—er—things in recent—
    ech—
in the United—If your screen is black,
ladies & gentlemen, we—I like—
at the Point he was already terrific—sick

to a second term, having done no wrong—
no right—no right—having let the Army—bang—
defend itself from Joe, let venom' Strauss
bile Oppenheimer out of use—use Robb,
who'll later fend for Goldfine—Breaking no laws,
he lay in the White House—sob!!—

who never understood his own strategy—whee—
so Monty's memoirs—nor any strategy,
wanting the ball bulled thro' all parts of the line
at once—proving, by his refusal to take Berlin,
he misread even Clauswitz—wide empty grin
that never lost a vote (O Adlai mine).

24

Oh servant Henry lectured till
the crows commenced and then
he bulbed his voice & lectured on some more.

This happened again & again, like war,—
the Indian p.a.'s, such as they were,
a weapon on his side, for the birds.

Vexations held a field-monsoon.
He was Introduced, and then he was Summed-up.
He was put questions on race bigotry;
he put no questions on race bigotry
constantly.
The mad sun rose though on the ghats
   & the saddhu in maha mudra, the great River,

and Henry was happy & beside him with excitement.
Beside himself, his possibilities;
salaaming hours of a half-blind morning
while the rainy lepers salaamed back,
smiles & a passion of their & his eyes flew
in feelings not ever accorded solely to oneself.

26

The glories of the world struck me, made me aria, once.
—What happen then, Mr Bones?
if be you cares to say.
—Henry. Henry became interested in women's bodies,
his loins were & were the   scene of stupendous
    achievement.
Stupor. Knees, dear. Pray.

All the knobs & softnesses of, my God,
the ducking & trouble it swarm on Henry,
at one time.
—What happen then, Mr Bones?
you seems excited-like.
—Fell Henry back into   the original crime: art, rime

besides a sense of others, my God, my God,
and a jealousy for the honour (alive) of his country,
what can get more odd?
and discontent with the thriving gangs & pride.
—What happen then, Mr Bones?
—I had a most marvellous   piece of luck. I died.

28
Snow Line

It was wet & white & swift and where I am
we don't know. It was dark and then
it isn't.
I wish the barker would come. There seems to be to eat
nothing. I am unusually tired.
I'm alone too.

If only the strange one with so few legs would come,
I'd say my prayers out of my mouth, as usual.
Where are his notes I loved?
There may be horribles; it's hard to tell.
The barker nips me but somehow I feel
he too is on my side.

I'm too alone. I see no end. If we could all
run, even that would be better. I am hungry.
The sun is not hot.
It's not a good position I am in.
If I had to do the whole thing over again
I wouldn't.

29

There sat down, once, a thing on Henry's heart
só heavy, if he had a hundred years
& more, & weeping, sleepless, in all them time
Henry could not make good.
Starts again always in Henry's ears
the little cough somewhere, an odour, a chime.

And there is another thing he has in mind
like a grave Sienese face a thousand years
would fail to blur the still profiled reproach of. Ghastly,
with open eyes, he attends, blind.
All the bells say: too late. This is not for tears;
thinking.

But never did Henry, as he thought he did,
end anyone and hacks her body up
and hide the pieces, where they may be found.
He knows: he went over everyone, & nobody's missing.
Often he reckons, in the dawn, them up.
Nobody is ever missing.

30

Collating bones: I would have liked to do.
Henry would have been hot at that.
I missed his profession.
As a little boy I always thought
'I'm an archeologist'; who
could be more respected peaceful serious than that?

Hell talkt my brain awake.
Bluffed to the ends of me pain
& I took up a pencil;
like this I'm longing with. One sign
would snow me back, back.
Is there anyone in the audience who has lived in vain?

A Chinese tooth! African jaw!
Drool, says a nervous system,
for a joyous replacing. Heat burns off dew.
Between the Ices (Mindel-Würm)
in a world I ever saw
some of my dying people indexed: "Warm."

34

My mother has your shotgun. One man, wide
in the mind, and tendoned like a grizzly, pried
to his trigger-digit, pal.
He should not have done that, but, I guess,
he didn't feel the best, Sister,—felt less
and more about less than us . . . ?

Now—tell me, my love, *if* you recall
the dove light after dawn at the island and all—
here is the story, Jack:
he verbed for forty years, very enough,
& shot & buckt—and, baby, there was of
schist but small there (some).

Why should I tell a truth? when in the crack
of the dooming & emptying news I did hold back—
in the taxi too, sick—
silent—it's so I broke down here, in his mind
whose sire as mine one same way—I refuse,
hoping the guy go home.

36

The high ones die, die. They die. You look up and who's
    there?
—Easy, easy, Mr Bones. I is on your side.
I smell your grief.
—I sent my grief away. I cannot care
forever. With them all again & again I died
and cried, and I have to live.

—Now there *you* exaggerate, Sah. We hafta *die*.
That is our 'pointed task. Love & die.
—Yes; that makes sense.
But what makes sense between, then? What if I
roiling & babbling & braining, brood on why and
just sat on the fence?

—I doubts you did or do. De choice is lost.
—It's fool's gold. But I go in for that.
The boy & the bear
looked at each other. Man all is tossed
& lost with groin-wounds by the grand bulls, cat.
William Faulkner's where?

(Frost being still around.)

37

Three Around the Old Gentleman

His malice was a pimple down his good
big face, with its sly eyes. I must be sorry
Mr Frost has left:
I like it so less I don't understood—
he couldn't hear or see well—all we sift—
but this is a *bad* story.

He had fine stories and was another man
in private; difficult, always. Courteous,
on the whole, in private.
He apologize to Henry, off & on,
for two blue slanders; which was good of him.
I don't know how he made it.

Quickly, off stage with all but kindness, now.
I can't say what I have in mind. Bless Frost,
any odd god around.

Gentle his shift, I decussate & command,
stoic deity. For a while here we possessed
an unusual man.

40

I'm scared a lonely. Never see my son,
easy be not to see anyone,
combers out to sea
know they're goin somewhere but not me.
Got a little poison, got a little gun,
I'm scared a lonely.

I'm scared a only one thing, which is me,
from othering I don't take nothin, see,
for any hound dog's sake.
But this is where I livin, where I rake
my leaves and cop my promise, this' where we
cry oursel's awake.

Wishin was dyin but I gotta make
it all this way to that bed on these feet
where peoples said to meet.
Maybe but even if I see my son
forever never, get back on the take,
free, black & forty-one.

41

If we sang in the wood (and Death is a German expert)
while snow flies, chill, after so frequent knew
so many all of nothing,
for lead & fire, it's not we would assert
particulars, but animal; cats mew,
horses scream, man sing.

Or: men psalm. Man palms his ears and moans.
Death is a German expert. Scrambling, sitting,
spattering, we hurry.
I try to. Odd & trivial, atones
somehow for *my* escape a bullet splitting
my trod-on instep, fiery.

The cantor bubbled, rattled. The Temple burned.
Lurch with me! phantoms of Varshava. Slop!
When I used to be,
who haunted, stumbling, sewers, my sacked shop,
roofs, a dis-world *ai!* Death was a German
home-country.

45

He stared at ruin. Ruin stared straight back.
He thought they was old friends. He felt on the stair
where her papa found them bare
they became familiar. When the papers were lost
rich with pals' secrets, he thought he had the knack
of ruin. Their paths crossed

and once they crossed in jail; they crossed in bed;
and over an unsigned letter their eyes met,
and in an Asian city
directionless & lurchy at two & three,
or trembling to a telephone's fresh threat,
and when some wired his head

to reach a wrong opinion, 'Epileptic'.
But he noted now that: they were not old friends.
He did not know this one.
This one was a stranger, come to make amends
for all the imposters, and to make it stick.
Henry nodded, un-.

46

I am, outside. Incredible panic rules.
People are blowing and beating each other without
        mercy.
Drinks are boiling. Iced
drinks are boiling. The worse anyone feels, the worse
treated he is. Fools elect fools.
A harmless man at an intersection said, under his
        breath: "Christ!"

That word, so spoken, affected the vision
of, when they trod to work next day, shopkeepers
who went & were fitted for glasses.
Enjoyed they then an appearance of love & law.
Millenia whiff & waft—one, one—er, er . . .
Their glasses were taken from them, & they saw.

Man has undertaken the top job of all,
son fin. Good luck.
I myself walked at the funeral of tenderness.
Followed other deaths. Among the last,
like the memory of a lovely fuck,
was: *Do, ut des*.

48

He yelled at me in Greek,
my God!—It's not his language
and I'm no good at—his is Aramaic,
was—I am a monoglot of English
(American version) and, say pieces from
a baker's dozen others: where's the bread?

but rising in the Second Gospel, pal:
The seed goes down, god dies,
a rising happens,
some crust, and then occurs   an eating. He said so,
a Greek idea,
troublesome to imaginary Jews,

like bitter Henry, full of the death of love,
Cawdor-uneasy, disambitious, mourning
the whole implausible necessary thing.
He dropped his voice & sybilled of
the death of the death of love.
I óught to get going.

50

In a motion of night they massed nearer my post.
I hummed a short blues. When the stars went out
I studied my weapons system.
Grenades, the portable rack, the yellow spout
of the anthrax-ray: in order. Yes, and most
of my pencils were sharp.

This edge of the galaxy has often seen
a defence so stiff, but it could only go
one way.
—Mr Bones, your troubles give me vertigo,
& backache. Somehow, when I make your scene,
I cave to feel as if

de roses of dawns & pearls of dusks, made up
by some ol' writer-man, got right forgot
& the greennesses of ours.
Springwater grow so thick it gonna clot
and the pleasing ladies cease. I figure, yup,
you is bad powers.

51

Our wounds to time, from all the other times,
sea-times slow, the times of galaxies
fleeing, the dwarfs' dead times,
lessen so little that if here in his crude rimes
Henry them mentions, do not hold it, please,
for a putting of man down.

Ol' Marster, being bound you do your best
versus we coons, spare now a cagey John
a whilom bits that whip:
who'll tell your fortune, when you have confessed
whose & whose woundings—against the innocent stars
& remorseless seas—

—Are you radioactive, pal? —Pal, radioactive.
—Has you the night sweats & the day sweats, pal?
—Pal, I do.
—Did your gal leave you? —What do *you* think, pal?
—Is that thing on the front of your head what it seems
    to be, pal?
—Yes, pal.

53

He lay in the middle of the world, and twitcht.
More Sparine for Pelides,
human (half) & down here as he is,
with probably insulting mail to open
and certainly unworthy words to hear
and his unforgivable memory.

—I seldom *go* to *films*. They are too exciting,
said the Honourable Possum.
—It takes me so long to read the 'paper,
said to me one day a novelist hot as a firecracker,
because I have to identify myself with everyone in it,
including the corpses, pal.'

Kierkegaard wanted a society, to refuse to read 'papers,
and that was not, friends, his worst idea.
Tiny Hardy, toward the end, refused to say *anything*,
a programme adopted early on by long Housman,
and Gottfried Benn
said:—We are using our own skins for wallpaper and we
    cannot win.

54

'NO VISITORS' I thumb the roller to
and leans against the door.
Comfortable in my horseblanket
I prop on the costly bed & dream of my wife,
my first wife,
and my second wife & my son.

Insulting, they put guardrails up,
as if it were a crib!
I growl at the head nurse; we compose on one.
I have been operating from *nothing*,
like a dog after its tail
more slowly, losing altitude.

Nitid. They are shooting me full of sings.
I give no rules. Write as short as you can,
in order, of what matters.
I think of my beloved poet
Issa & his father who
sat down on the grass and took leave of each other.

55

Peter's not friendly. He gives me sideways looks.
The architecture is far from reassuring.
I feel uneasy.
A pity,—the interview began so well:
I mentioned fiendish things, he waved them away
and sloshed out a martini

strangely needed. We spoke of indifferent matters—
God's health, the vague hell of the Congo,
John's energy,
anti-matter matter. I felt fine.
Then a change came backward. A chill fell.
Talk slackened,

died, and he began to give me sideways looks.
'Christ,' I thought 'what now?' and would have askt for
        another
but didn't dare.
I feel my application   failing. It's growing dark,
some other sound is overcoming. His last words are:
'We betrayed me.'

Bats have no bankers and they do not drink
and cannot be arrested and pay no tax
and, in general, bats have it made.
Henry for joining the human race is *bats*,
known to be so, by few them who think,
out of the cave.

Instead of the cave! ah lovely-chilly, dark,
ur-moist his cousins hang in hundreds or swerve
with personal radar,
crisisless, kid. Instead of the cave? I serve,
inside, my blind term. Filthy four-foot lights
reflect on the whites of our eyes.

He then salutes for sixty years of it
just now a one of valor and insights,
a theatrical man,
O scholar & Legionnaire who as quickly might
have killed as cast you. *Olè*. Stormed with years
he tranquil commands and appears.

67

I don't operate often. When I do,
persons take note.
Nurses look amazed. They pale.
The patient is brought back to life, or so.
The reason I don't do this more (I quote)
is: I have a living to fail—

because of my wife & son—to keep from earning.
—Mr Bones, I sees that.
They for these operations thanks you, what?
not pays you. —Right.
You have seldom been so understanding.
Now there is further a difficulty with the light:

I am obliged to perform in complete darkness
operations of great delicacy
on my self.
—Mr Bones, you terrifies me.
No wonder they don't pay you. Will you die?
—My
        friend, I succeeded. Later.

68

I heard, could be, a Hey there from the wing,
and I went on: Miss Bessie soundin good
that one, that night of all,
I feelin fair mysef, taxes & things
seem to be back in line, like everybody should
and nobody in the snow on call

so, as I say, the house is givin hell
to *Yellow Dog*, I blowin like it too
and Bessie always do
when she make a very big sound—after, well,
no sound—I see she totterin—I cross which stage
even at Henry's age

in 2–3 seconds: then we wait and see.
I hear strange horns, Pinetop he hit some chords,
Charlie start *Empty Bed*,
they all come hangin Christmas on some tree
after trees thrown out—sick-house's white birds',
black to the birds instead.

69

Love her he doesn't but the thought he puts
into that young woman
would launch a national product
complete with TV spots & skywriting
outlets in Bonn & Tokyo
I mean it

Let it be known that nine words have not passed
between herself and Henry;
looks, smiles.
God help Henry, who deserves it all
every least part of that infernal & unconscious
woman, and the pain.

I feel as if, unique, she . . . Biddable?
Fates, conspire.
—Mr Bones, *please*.
—Vouchsafe me, Sleepless One,
a personal experience of the body of Mrs Boogry
before I pass from lust!

70

Disengaged, bloody, Henry rose from the shell
where in their racing start his seat got wedged
under his knifing knees,
he did it on the runners, feathering,
being bow, catching no crab. The ridges were sore
& tore chamois. It was not done with ease.

So Henry was a hero, malgré lui,
that day, for blundering; until & after the coach
said this & which to him.
That happy day, whenas the pregnant back
of Number Two returned, and he'd no choice
but to make for it room.

Therefore he rowed rowed rowed. They did not win.
Forever in the winning & losing since
of his own crew, or rather
in the weird regattas of this afterworld,
cheer for the foe. He set himself to time
the blue father.

75

Turning it over, considering, like a madman
Henry put forth a book.
No harm resulted from this.
Neither the menstruating   stars (nor man) was moved
at once.
Bare dogs drew closer for a second look

and performed their friendly operations there.
Refreshed, the bark rejoiced.
Seasons went and came.
Leaves fell, but only a few.
Something remarkable about this
unshedding bulky bole-proud blue-green moist

thing made by savage & thoughtful
surviving Henry
began to strike the passers from despair
so that sore on their shoulders old men hoisted
six-foot sons and polished women called
small girls to dream awhile toward the flashing &
    bursting tree!

⁷⁶
Henry's Confession

Nothin very bad happen to me lately.
How you explain that? —I explain that, Mr Bones,
terms o' your bafflin odd sobriety.
Sober as man can get, no girls, no telephones,
what could happen bad to Mr Bones?
—*If* life is a handkerchief sandwich,

in a modesty of death I join my father
who dared so long agone leave me.
A bullet on a concrete stoop
close by a smothering southern sea
spreadeagled on an island, by my knee.
—You is from hunger, Mr Bones,

I offers you this handkerchief, now set
your left foot by my right foot,
shoulder to shoulder, all that jazz,

arm in arm, by the beautiful sea,
hum a little, Mr Bones.
—I saw nobody coming, so I went instead.

77

Seedy Henry rose up shy in de world
& shaved & swung his barbells, duded Henry up
and p.a.'d poor thousands of persons on topics of grand
moment to Henry, ah to those less & none.
Wif a book of his in either hand
he is stript down to move on.

—Come away, Mr Bones.

—Henry is tired of the winter,
& haircuts, & a squeamish comfy   ruin-prone proud
        national mind,   & Spring (in the city so called).
Henry likes Fall.
Hé would be prepared to líve in a world of Fáll
for ever, impenitent Henry.
But the snows and summers grieve & dream;

thése fierce & airy occupations, and love,
raved away so many of Henry's years
it is a wonder that, with in each hand
one of his own mad books and all,
ancient fires for eyes, his head full
& his heart full, he's making ready to move on.

78
Op. posth. no. 1

Darkened his eye, his wild smile disappeared,
inapprehensible his studies grew,
nourished he less & less
his subject body with good food & rest,
something bizarre about Henry, slowly sheared
off, unlike you & you,

smaller & smaller, till in question stood
his eyeteeth and one block of memories
These were enough for him
implying commands from upstairs & from down,
Walt's 'orbic flex,' triads of Hegel would
incorporate, if you please,

into the know-how of the American bard
embarrassed Henry heard himself a-being,
and the younger Stephen Crane
of a powerful memory, of pain,
these stood the ancestors, relaxed & hard,
whilst Henry's parts were fleeing.

79

Op. posth. no. 2

Whence flew the litter whereon he was laid?
Of what heroic stuff was warlock Henry made?
and questions of that sort
perplexed the bulging cosmos, O in short
was sandalwood in good supply when he
flared out of history

& the obituary in *The New York Times*
into the world of generosity
creating the air where are
& can be, only, heroes? Statues & rhymes
signal his fiery Passage, a mountainous sea,
the occlusion of a star:

anything afterward, of high lament,
let too his giant faults appear, as sent
together with his virtues down
and let this day be his, throughout the town,
region & cosmos, lest he freeze our blood
with terrible returns.

Op. posth. no. 14

Noises from underground made gibber some,
others collected & dug Henry up
saying 'You *are* a sight.'
Chilly, he muttered for a double rum
waving the mikes away, putting a stop
to rumours, pushing his fright

off with the now accumulated taxes
accustomed in his way to solitude
and no bills.
Wives came forward, claiming a new Axis,
fearful for their insurance, though, now, glued
to disencumbered Henry's many ills.

A fortnight later, sense a single man
upon the trampled scene at 2 a.m.
insomnia-plagued, with a shovel
digging like mad, Lazarus with a plan
to get his own back, a plan, a stratagem
no newsman will unravel.

General Fatigue stalked in, & a Major-General,
Captain Fatigue, and at the base of all
pale Corporal Fatigue,
and curious microbes came, came viruses:

and the Court conferred on Henry, and conferred on
     Henry
the rare Order of Weak.

—How come dims *one* these wholesome elsers oh?
Old polymaths, old trackers, far from home,
say how thro' auburn hair   titbits of youth's grey climb.
I have heard of rose-cheekt but the rose is here!
I bell: when pops her phiz in   a good crow.
My beauty is off duty!—

Henry relives a lady, how down vain,
spruce in her succinct parts, spruce everywhere.
They fed like muscles and lunched
after, between, before. He tracks her, hunched
(propped on red table elbows) at her telephone,
white rear bare in the air.

143

—That's enough of that, Mr Bones. *Some* lady you
     make.
Honour the burnt cork, be a vaudeville man,
I'll sing you now a song
the like of which may bring your heart to break:
he's gone! and we don't know where. When he began
taking the pistol out & along,

you was just a little; but gross fears
accompanied us along the beaches, pal.

My mother was scared almost to death.
He was going to swim out, with me, forevers,
and a swimmer strong he was in the
      phosphorescent   Gulf,
but he decided on lead.

That mad drive wiped out my childhood. I put him
      down
while all the same on forty years I love him
stashed in Oklahoma
besides his brother Will. Bite the nerve of the town
for anyone so desperate. I repeat: I love him
until *I* fall into coma.

145

Also I love him: me he's done no wrong
for going on forty years—forgiveness time—
I touch now his despair,
he felt as bad as Whitman on his tower
but he did not swim out with me or my brother
as he threatened—

a powerful swimmer, to   take one of us along
as company in the defeat sublime,
freezing my helpless mother:
he only, very early in the morning,
rose with his gun and went outdoors by my window
and did what was needed.

I cannot read that wretched mind, so strong
& so undone. I've always tried. I—I'm
trying to forgive
whose frantic passage, when he could not live
an instant longer, in the summer dawn
left Henry to live on.

147

Henry's mind grew blacker the more he thought.
He looked onto the world like the act of an aged whore.
Delmore, Delmore.
He flung to pieces and they hit the floor.
Nothing was true but what Marcus Aurelius taught,
'All that is foul smell & blood in a bag.'

He lookt on the world like the leavings of a hag.
Almost his love died from him, any more.
His mother & William
were vivid in the same mail Delmore died.
The world is lunatic. This is the last ride.
Delmore, Delmore.

High in the summer branches the poet sang.
Hís throat ached, and he could sing no more.
All ears closed
across the heights where Delmore & Gertrude sprang
so long ago, in the goodness of which it was composed.
Delmore, Delmore!

Glimmerings

His hours of thought grew longer, his study less,
the data (he decided) were abundantly his,
or if not, never.
He called on old codes or new apperceptions,
he fought off an anxiety attack as the Lord did nations,
with brutal commitments, not clever.

Almost he lost interest in the 14 books part-done
in favour of insights fresh, a laziness in the sun,
rapid sketchings,
a violent level on the drop of friendship,
'I am pickt up & sorted to a pip,'
sleepless, watching.

Gravediggers all busy, Jelly, look what you done done
there died of late a great cat, a real boss cat
fallen from his prime
I'm sorry for those coming, I'm sorry for everyone
At least my friend is   rid of that
for the present space-time.

He had followers but they could not find him;
friends but they could not find him. He hid his gift
in the center of Manhattan,
without a girl, in cheap hotels,

so disturbed on the street friends avoided him
Where did he come by his lift

which all we must or we would rapidly die:
did he remember the more beautiful & fresh poems
of early manhood now?
or did his subtle & strict standards allow
them nothing, baffled? What then did self-love show
of the weaker later, somehow?

I'd bleed to say his lovely work improved
but it is not so. He painfully removed
himself from the ordinary contacts
and shook with resentment. What final thought
solaced his fall to the hotel carpet, if any,
& the *New York Times*'s facts?

151

Bitter & bleary over Delmore's dying:
his death stopped clocks, let no activity
mar our hurrah of mourning,
let's all be Jews bereft, for he was one
He died too soon, he liked 'An Ancient to Ancients'
His death clouded the grove

I need to hurry this out before I forget
which I will never   He fell on the floor
outside a cheap hotel-room

my tearducts are worn out, the ambulance came
and there on the way he died
He was 'smart & kind,'

a child's epitaph. He had no children,
nobody to stand by in the awful years
of the failure of his administration
He was tortured, beyond what man might be
Sick & heartbroken Henry sank to his knees
Delmore is dead. His good body lay unclaimed
three days.

152
I bid you then a raggeder farewell
than at any time my grief would have desired,
you take secrets with you,
sudden appearances, and worse to tell,
vanishings. You said 'My head's on fire'
meaning inspired O

meeting on the walk down to Warren House
so long ago we were almost anonymous
waiting for fame to descend
with a scarlet mantle & tell us who we were.
Young poets are ridiculous, and rare
like a man death-wounded on the mend.

There's a memorial today at N.Y.U.,
your last appearance, old heroic friend.

I hope the girls are pretty
and the remarks radish-crisp befitting you
to allay the horror of your lonely end,
appease, a little, sorrow & pity.

153

I'm cross with god who has wrecked this generation.
First he seized Ted, then Richard, Randall, and now
     Delmore.
In between he gorged on Sylvia Plath.
That was a first rate haul. He left alive
fools I could number like a kitchen knife
but Lowell he did not touch.

Somewhere the enterprise continues, not—
yellow the sun lies on the baby's blouse—
in Henry's staggered thought.
I suppose the word would be, we must submit.
Later.
I hang, and I will not be part of it.

A friend of Henry's contrasted God's career
with Mozart's, leaving Henry with nothing to say
but praise for a word so apt.
We suffer on, a day, a day, a day.
And never again can come, like a man slapped,
news like this

155

I can't get him out of my mind, out of my mind,
Hé was out of his own mind for years,
in police stations & Bellevue.
He drove up to my house in Providence
ho ho at 8 a.m. in a Cambridge taxi
and told it to wait.

He walked my living-room, & did not want breakfast
or even coffee, or even even a drink.
He paced, I'd say Sit down,
it makes me nervous, for a moment he'd sit down,
then pace. After an hour or so *I* had a drink.
He took it back to Cambridge,

we never learnt why he came, or what he wanted.
His mission was obscure. His mission was real,
but obscure.
I remember his electrical insight as the young man,
his wit & passion, gift, the whole young man
alive with surplus love.

156

I give in. I must not leave   the scene of this same death
as most of me strains to.
There are all the problems to be sorted out,
the fate of the soul, what it was all about
during its being, and whether he was drunk
at 4 a.m. on the wrong floor too

fighting for air, tearing his sorry clothes
with his visions dying O and O I mourn
again this complex death
Almost my oldest friend should never have been born
to this terrible end, out of which what grows
but an unshaven, disheveled *corpse*?

The spirit & the joy, in memory
live of him on, the young will read his young verse
for as long as such things go:
why then do I despair, miserable Henry
who *knew* him all so long, for better & worse
and nearly would follow him below.

159

Panic & shock, together. They are all going away.
Henry took down his black four-in-hand & his black
      bowtie
and put away all other ties.
It is a pleasant Sunday summer afternoon,
I have been sick five times. Can I go on?
I am a half-closed book.

Exalted figures passed before Henry's eyes,
passed & withdrew. Retaining his faculties
barely, his trajectory,
his heart still beating in his empty breast,
he hollow-hearted waved to them going by
& out of sight.

I feel a final chill. This is cold sweat
that will not leave me now. Maybe it's time
to throw in my own hand.
But there are secrets, secrets, I may yet—
hidden in history & theology, hidden in rhyme—
come on to understand.

192

Love me love me love me love me love me
I am in need thereof, I mean of love,
I married her.
That was a hasty & a violent step
like an unhopeful Kierkegardian leap,
wasn't it, dear?

Slowly the sloth moved on in search of prey,
I see that. The jungles flash with light,
in some angles dark as midnight,
and chuck chuck chuck the spark did make a noise
when he cross the street on de electric wires
but that sloth was all right.

Swiftly the wind rose, gorgons showed their teeth,
while the bombs bombed on empty territory beneath.
I love you.
Will I forget ever my sole guru
far in Calcutta. I do not think so.
Nor will I you.

Tears Henry shed for poor old Hemingway
Hemingway in despair, Hemingway at the end,
the end of Hemingway,
tears in a diningroom in Indiana
and that was years ago, before his marriage say,
God to him no worse luck send.

Save us from shotguns & fathers' suicides.
It all depends on who you're the father *of*
if you want to kill yourself—
a bad example, murder of oneself,
the final death, in a paroxysm, of love
for which good mercy hides?

A girl at the door: 'A few coppers pray'
But to return, to return to Hemingway
that cruel & gifted man.
Mercy! my father; do not pull the trigger
or all my life I'll suffer from your anger
killing what you began.

Am I a bad man? Am I a good man?
—Hard to say, Brother Bones. Maybe you both,
like most of we.
—The evidence is difficult to structure towards
    deliberate evil.
But what of the rest? Does it wax for wrath
in its infinite complexity?

She left without a word, for Ecuador.
I would have liked to discuss more with her this thing
through the terrible nights.
She was than Henry wiser, being younger or
a woman. She brought me Sanka and violent drugs
which were yet wholly inadequate.

My doctor doubles them daily. Am I a bad one—
I'm thinking of them fires & their perplexness—
or may a niche be found
in nothingness for completely exhausted Henry?
But it comes useless to canvass this alone,
out of her eyes and sound.

279

Leaving behind the country of the dead
where he must then return & die himself
he set his tired face due East
where the sun rushes up the North Atlantic
and where had paused a little the war for bread
& the war for status had ceased

forever, and he took with him five books,
a Whitman & a Purgatorio,
a one-volume dictionary,
an Oxford Bible with all its bays & nooks
& bafflements long familiar to Henry
& one other new book-O.

If ever he had crafted in the past—
but only if—he swore now to craft better
which lay in the Hands above.
He said: I'll work on slow, O slow & fast,
if a letter comes I will answer that letter
& my whole year will be tense with love.

327

Freud was some wrong about dreams, or almost all;
besides his insights grand, he thought that dreams were
     a transcript
of childhood & the day before,
censored of course: *a* transcript:
even his lesser insight were misunderstood & became a
     bore
except for the knowing & troubled by the Fall.

Grand Jewish ruler, custodian of the past,
our paedegogue to whip us into truth,
I sees your long story,
tyrannical & triumphant all-wise at last
you wholly failed to take into account youth
& had no interest in your glory.

I tell you, Sir, you have enlightened but
you have misled us: a dream is a panorama
of the whole mental life,

I took one once to forty-three structures, that
accounted in each for each word: I did not yell 'mama'
nor did I take it out on my wife.

350

All the girls, with their vivacious littles,
visited him in dream: he was interested in their tops &
        bottoms
& even in their middles,
for years Henry had been getting away with *murder*,
the Sheriff mused. There'll have to be an order
specifically to stop climbing trees,

& other people's wives: we'll cut off his telephone,
stroke one, and hasten his senility,
stroke two: encourage his virtues, if he has one:
ask him upstairs more frequently for tea,
stroke four, put him on the wagon, Death,
no drinks: that ought to cure him.

The progress of age helped him, to be not good but
        better:
he restricted his passes to passes made by letters
he drank less.
Mlle Choinais noted a definite though small improve-
        ment in Henry:
as they passed forth across the northern sea,
a degree of gentleness.

The only happy people in the world
are those who do not have   to write long poems:
muck, administration, toil:
the protototality of an absence of contact
in one's own generation, chiefly the old & the young
persisting with interest.

'The Care & Feeding of Long Poems' was Henry's title
for his next essay, which will come out when
he wants it to.
A Kennedy-sponsored bill for the protection
of poets from long poems   will benefit the culture
and do no harm to that kind Lady, Mrs Johnson.

He would have gone to the White House & consulted
     the President
during his 10 seconds in the receiving line
on the problems of long poems
Mr Johnson has never written one
but he seems a generous & able man
'Tetelestai' said St John.

Chilled in this Irish pub I wish my loves
well, well to strangers, well to all his friends,
seven or so in number,
I forgive my enemies, especially two,
races his heart, at so much magnanimity,
can it at all be true?

—Mr Bones, you on a trip outside yourself.
Has you seen a medicine man? You sound will-like,
a testament & such.
Is you going?—Oh, I suffer from a strike
& a strike & three balls: I stand up for much,
Wordsworth & that sort of thing.

The pitcher dreamed. He threw a hazy curve,
I took it in my stride & out I struck,
lonesome Henry.
These Songs are not meant to be understood, you
    understand.
They are only meant to terrify & comfort.
Lilac was found in his hand.

381

Cave-man Henry grumbled to his spouse
'It's cold in here. I'd rather have a house.
A house would be better.'
The bear-robe did them fairly well, but still
they certainly might fall ill.
I'm writing Mr Antelope a letter.

Leslie we lost all down the pure rock-face
& that was terrifying. Junior tried a trip in space
& ever since then he'll stutter.
I woke our wiseman over an awful dream:
vividest his shrew-spouse: Scream.
I'm writing Mr Antelope a letter.

And with great good luck I'll say a little more.
I am frightened by the waves upon the shore,
& seldom steal there, wetter
with the wild rain but safe, & back to the cave.
What he rendered forward too he forgave.
I'm writing Mr Antelope a letter.

382

At Henry's bier let some thing fall out well:
enter there none who somewhat has to sell,
the music ancient & gradual,
the voices solemn but the grief subdued,
no hairy jokes but everybody's mood
subdued, subdued,

until the Dancer comes, in a short short dress
hair black & long & loose, dark dark glasses,
uptilted face,
pallor & strangeness, the music changes
to 'Give!' & 'Ow!' and how! the music changes,
she kicks a backward limb

on tiptoe, pirouettes, & she is free
to the knocking music, sails, dips, & suddenly
returns to the terrible gay
occasion hopeless & mad, she weaves, it's hell,
she flings to her head a leg, bobs, all is well,
she dances Henry away.

384

The marker slants, flowerless, day's almost done,
I stand above my father's grave with rage,
often, often before
I've made this awful pilgrimage to one
who cannot visit me, who tore his page
out: I come back for more,

I spit upon this dreadful banker's grave
who shot his heart out in a Florida dawn
O ho alas alas
When will indifference come, I moan & rave
I'd like to scrabble till I got right down
away down under the grass

and ax the casket open ha to see
just how he's taking it, which he sought so hard
we'll tear apart
the mouldering grave clothes ha & then Henry
will heft the ax once more, his final card,
and fell it on the start.

385

My daughter's heavier. Light leaves are flying.
Everywhere in enormous numbers turkeys will be dying
and other birds, all their wings.
They never greatly flew. Did they wish to?
I should know. Off away somewhere once I knew
such things.

Or good Ralph Hodgson back then did, or does.
The man is dead whom Eliot praised. My praise
follows and flows too late.
Fall is grievy, brisk. Tears behind the eyes
almost fall. Fall comes to us as a prize
to rouse us toward our fate.

My house is made of wood and it's made well,
unlike us. My house is older than Henry;
that's fairly old.
If there were a middle   ground between things and the
      soul
or if the sky resembled more the sea,
I wouldn't have to scold

                        my heavy daughter.

Freshman Blues

My intense friend was tall & strongly made,
almost too handsome—& he was afraid
his penis was too small.
We mooted it, we did everything but examine it

whether *in se* or by comparison
to the great red joy a pecker ought to be
to pump a woman ragged. Only kid sisters,
he muttered, want to somersault with me.

Thought much I then on perforated daddy,
daddy boxed in & let down with strong straps,
when I my friends' homes visited, with fathers
universal & intact.

McGovern was critical: I treated my girl *slight*
who was so kind to me I climbed in bed
with her, with our pajamas, an icy morning
when I'd stayed overnight

by her mother's kindness, flustered by my status,
listening then downstairs.
Tom took her over and I ceased to fear
her nervous & carbuncled brother Thornton.

Nowhere

Traitoring *words*,—tearing my thought across
bearing it to foes.
Two men ahead of me in line in the College Study
about the obscurity of my 'Elegy: Hart Crane'.

More comfortable at the Apollo among blacks
than in Hartley Hall where I hung out.
A one named Brooks Johnson, with it in for Negroes,
I told one noon I'd some coon blood myself

and he spread the word wide while the campus laughed.
Magical mourning blues, at the Apollo & on records.
Victoria, Bessie. Teagarden. Pine-top Smith
the sightless passionate constructor.

Anti-semitism through the purblind Houses.
News weird out of Germany.
Our envy for any visitor to the Soviet Union.
The shaking incredible transcripts of the Trials.

Cagney's inventions in gesture, the soul-kiss
in *42nd Street*. Coop's little-boy-ness.
Chaplin emerging nonchalant from under the tarpaulin.
Five Dietrich films in a day.

Ping-pong at the Little Carnegie,
the cheapest firstrate date in the Depression city.
A picture of me in *The New York Times*
with a jock-strap on, & socks & shoes,

taken during the Freshman-Sophomore Rush:
face full from the camera, hardly any knew me,
praise God in St Bonaventura's Heaven!
Hours of acedia, pencil on the desk

coffee in a cup, ash-tray flowing
the window closed, the universe unforthcoming,
Being ground to a halt.
Inaccessible unthinkable the childlike enthusiasm

of grand Unamuno setting down his profession
in the Visitors' Book on top of a Spanish mountain:
'A humble man, & a tramp'.
Long after, in a train from Avila

I met a cop who called him Don Miguel;
another of my Sophomore heroes.
And David Hume stood high with me that year
& Kleist, for the 'Puppet-theatre'.

Uncertainties, presentiments.
Piranesi's black & lovely labyrinths, come-ons like a
    whore's.
Gautier rapt before a staircase at the Alcázar
winding up monumental through the ruin to give out
    on—nothing.

The Heroes

For all his vehemence & hydraulic opinions
Pound seemed feline, zeroing in on feelings,
hovering up to them, putting his tongue in their ear,
delicately modulating them in & out of each other.

Almost supernatural crafter; maybe unhappy,
disappointed continually,
not fated like his protégé Tom or drunky Jim
or hard-headed Willie for imperial sway.

How I maneuvered in my mind their rôles
of administration for the modern soul
in English, now one, now ahead another,
for this or that special strength, wilful & sovereign.

I had, from my beginning, to adore heroes
& I elected that they witness to,
show forth, transfigure: life-suffering & pure heart
& hardly definable but central weaknesses

for which they were to be enthroned & forgiven by me.
They had to come on like revolutionaries,
enemies throughout to accident & chance,
relentless travellers, long used to failure

in tasks that but for them would sit like hanging judges
on faithless & by no means up to it Man.
Humility & complex pride their badges,
every 'third thought' their grave.

These gathering reflexions, against young women
against seven courses in my final term,
I couldn't sculpt into my helpless verse yet.
I wrote mostly about death.

Recovery

I don't know what the hell happened all that summer.
I was done in, mentally. I wrote nothing, I read nothing.
I spent a pot of money, not being used to money,
I forget on what, now. I felt dazed.

After some wandering days in Montreal
I went to a little town where Dr Locke
cured any & everything with foot 'adjustments',
on hundreds of patients daily from all over North
  America

outdoors in a hardwood grove in front of his clinic.
I made vague friends with a couple, the brother in a
  wheel-chair,
his pleasant sister looking after him.
They were dull & very poor. I gave them tea,

we talked about what young people talk about.
Weeks somehow went by. All this time my art was in
  escrow,
I vegetated, I didn't even miss Jean,
without interest in what I was, what I might become

never came up, as day by day
I stood in line for the Doctor & gave them tea.
I didn't think much of the nothing I knew of Canada,
half British-oriented, half-French, half-American;

no literature, painting, architecture,
music, philosophy, scholarship . . .
(McLuhan & Frye unthinkable ahead).
I wasn't unhappy, I wasn't anything,
until I pulled myself reluctantly together at last

& bowed goodbye to my lame ducks
& headed for Pier 42—where my nervous system
as I teetered across the gang-plank
sprang back into expectation. I kissed Jean

& Mother & shook hands with old Halliday
and I mounted to the *Britannic*'s topmost deck
O a young American poet, not yet good,
off to the strange Old World to pick their brains
& visit by hook or crook with W. B. Yeats.

Have a Genuine American Horror-&-Mist on the Rocks

(14,500 six-ton concrete-&-steel vaults of nerve-gas rockets, lethal)

The terrible trains crawl seaward thro' the South,
where TV teams quiz small-town citizens:
'Waal . . if the Army says it's safe, it's okay with me.
Ah've got a boy in Veetnam.'

All this mad stuff has been there fifteen years!
leaking its coffins. Had the Chinese come
down in Korea, who knows? then or now knows?
Nobody *knows anything*

but somewhere up in the murky constellation
of Government & the scientists & the military
responsible to no-one someone knows
that he too doesn't know anything

and can't say what would then have happened or will
        'now' *happen*
on the Atlantic bottom in the long dark
of decades of ecology to come
while the 20th Century flies insanely on.

Of Suicide

Reflexions on suicide, & on my father, possess me.
I drink too much. My wife threatens separation.
She won't 'nurse' me. She feels 'inadequate'.
We don't mix together.

It's an hour later in the East.
I could call up Mother in Washington, D.C.
But could she help me?
And all this postal adulation & reproach?

A basis rock-like of love & friendship
for all this world-wide madness seems to be needed.
Epictetus is in some ways my favourite philosopher.
Happy men have died earlier.

I still plan to go to Mexico this summer.
The Olmec images! Chichén Itzá!
D. H. Lawrence has a wild dream of it.
Malcolm Lowry's book when it came out I taught to my
      precept at Princeton.

I don't entirely resign. I may teach the Third Gospel
this afternoon. I haven't made up my mind.
It seems to me sometimes that others have easier jobs
& do them worse.

Well, we must labour & dream. Gogol was impotent,
somebody in Pittsburgh told me.
I said: At what age? They couldn't answer.
That is a damned serious matter.

Rembrandt was sober. There we differ. Sober.
Terrors came on him. To us too they come.
Of suicide I continually think.
Apparently he didn't. I'll teach Luke.

The Hell Poem

Hospital racket, nurses' iron smiles.
Jill & Eddie Jane are the souls.
I like nearly all the rest of them too
except when they feed me paraldehyde.

Tyson has been here three heavy months;
heroin. We have the same doctor: She's improving,
let out on pass tonight for her first time.
A madonna's oval face with wide dark eyes.

Everybody is jolly, patients, nurses,
orderlies, some psychiatrists. Anguishes;
gnawings. Protractions of return
to the now desired but frightful outer world.

Young Tyson hasn't eaten since she came back.
She went to a wedding, her mother harangued her
it was all much too much for her
she sipped wine with a girl-friend, she fled here.

Many file down for shock & can't say after
whether they ate breakfast. Dazed till four.
One word is: the memory will come back.
Ah, weeks or months. Maybe.

Behind the locked door, called 'back there',
the worse victims.
Apathy or ungovernable fear
cause them not to watch through the window starlight.

They can't have matches, or telephone. They slob food.
Tantrums, & the suicidal, are put back there.
Sometimes one is promoted here. We are ecstatic.
Sometimes one has to go back.

It's all girls this time. The elderly, the men,
of my former stays have given way to girls,
fourteen to forty, raucous, racing the halls,
cursing their paramours & angry husbands.

Nights of witches: I dreamt a headless child.
Sobbings, a scream, a slam.
Will day glow again to these tossers, and to me?
I am staying days.

Death Ballad

(*'I don't care'*)

Tyson & Jo, Tyson & Jo
became convinced it was no go
& decided to end it all
at nineteen,—on the psychiatric ward.

Trouble is, Tyson was on the locked ward,
Jo for some reason on the open
and they were forbidden to communicate
either their love or their hate.

Heroin & the cops were Tyson's bit
I don't know just what Jo's was, ah but it
was more self-destructive still.
She tried to tear a window & screen out.

United in their feel of worthlessness
& rage, they stood like sisters in their way
blocking their path. They made a list
of the lies of Society & glared: 'We don't exist.'

The charismatic quality of these charming & sensitive
    girls
smiled thro' their vices; all were fond of them
& wished them well.
They sneered: 'We prefer Hell.'

What will their fates be? Put their heads together,
in their present mental weather,
no power can prevent their dying. That is so.
Only, Jo & Tyson, Tyson & Jo,

take up, outside your blocked selves, some small thing
that is moving
& wants to keep on moving
& needs therefore, Tyson, Jo, your loving.

Heaven

Free! while in the cathedral at Seville
a Cardinal is singing. I bowed my face
& licked the monument. Aged women
waited behind me. Free! to lick & believe,

Free free! on an Easter afternoon
I almost said I loved her, we held hands
in the cemetery. Choirs came down on us,
St Anselm bothered his ecstatic repose to chide.

Ambrose interpreted: I was in love with her,
she was half with me. Among the tombs.
She was killed in a car accident soon after she married,
a lissom light-haired alluring phantastic young lady.

Fly by, spirits of Night, her cenotaph
& forgive my survival with one shoe.
She forgave me that golden day my lust for her
but what might persuade me to forgive her loss?

Allow her exalted kind forbidding voice
a place in the *Lachrymosa*.
Let her sing on.
O lucky spirits to sing on with her.

Then a *capella*: mourning, barely heard,
across the Venetian waters: louder, dear,
I have a 15% hearing loss from a childhood illness,
louder, my darling, over at San Giorgio.

The Home Ballad

We must work & play and John Jacob Niles
will sing our souls to rest
(in his earlier-78 recordings).
Tomorrow we'll do our best, our best,
tomorrow we'll do our best.

The income tax is done, is done,
and three full weeks before
& it's going to be O very bad
but the medical expenses are more, are more,
the medical & support are more.

I left the place with one cracked toe,
at noon I packed in haste
out of that hospital O to go
they wanted me to stay, to stay
for an X-ray. I said 'Doctors, pray

the thing's not dislocated or broken O
any damned thing beside—
if it is, you're helpless—if it's not, you're a bore'
O I left that ward on my right foot
lurching on my left toe.

It hurt like hell, but never mind—
I hobbled on to free
swinging my typescript book like a bee
with honey back to the comb, the comb,
bringing my lovelies home.

The postal strike will end, will end,
I sent that Nixon a wire
because my ex-wife said I should—
I always do what she says, she says,
because my son sets me on fire.

It's home to my daughter I am come
with verses & stories true,
which I would also share with you,
my dear, my dear,
only you are not my daughter.

Now my book will go to friends—
women & men of wit—
Xerox'd before we publish it, it,
the limited edition & the public it,
before we publish it.

It's *Love & Fame* called, honey Kate,
you read it from the start
and sometimes I reel when you praise my art
my honey almost hopeless angry art,
which was both our Fate—

from **Eleven Addresses to the Lord**

1

Master of beauty, craftsman of the snowflake,
inimitable contriver,
endower of Earth so gorgeous & different from the
  boring Moon,
thank you for such as it is my gift.

I have made up a morning prayer to you
containing with precision everything that most matters.
'According to Thy will' the thing begins.
It took me off & on two days. It does not aim at
  eloquence.

You have come to my rescue again & again
in my impassable, sometimes despairing years.
You have allowed my brilliant friends to destroy
  themselves
and I am still here, severely damaged, but functioning.

Unknowable, as I am unknown to my guinea pigs:
how can I 'love' you?
I only as far as gratitude & awe
confidently & absolutely go.

I have no idea whether we live again.
It doesn't seem likely
from either the scientific or the philosophical point of
  view
but certainly all things are possible to you,

and I believe as fixedly in the Resurrection-appearances
     to Peter & to Paul
as I believe I sit in this blue chair.
Only that may have been a special case
to establish their initiatory faith.

Whatever your end may be, accept my amazement.
May I stand until death forever at attention
for any your least instruction or enlightenment.
I even feel sure you will assist me again, Master of
     insight & beauty.

3

Sole watchman of the flying stars, guard me
against my flicker of impulse lust: teach me
to see them as sisters & daughters. Sustain
my grand endeavours: husbandship & crafting.

Forsake me not when my wild hours come;
grant me sleep nightly, grace soften my dreams;
achieve in me patience till the thing be done,
a careful view of my achievement come.

Make me from time to time the gift of the shoulder.
When all hurt nerves whine shut away the whiskey.
Empty my heart toward Thee.
Let me pace without fear the common path of death.

Cross am I sometimes with my little daughter:
fill her eyes with tears. Forgive me, Lord.
Unite my various soul,
sole watchman of the wide & single stars.

6

Under new management, Your Majesty:
Thine. I have solo'd mine since childhood, since
my father's suicide when I was twelve
blew out my most bright candle faith, and look at me.

I served at Mass six dawns a week from five,
adoring Father Boniface & you,
memorizing the Latin he explained.
Mostly we worked alone. One or two women.

Then my poor father frantic. Confusions & afflictions
followed my days. Wives left me.
Bankrupt I closed my doors. You pierced the roof
twice & again. Finally you opened my eyes.

My double nature fused in that point of time
three weeks ago day before yesterday.
Now, brooding thro' a history of the early Church,
I identify with everybody, even the heresiarchs.

A Prayer for the Self

Who am I worthless that You spent such pains
and take may pains again?
I do not understand; but I believe.
Jonquils respond with wit to the teasing breeze.

Induct me down my secrets. Stiffen this heart
to stand their horrifying cries, O cushion
the first the second shocks, will to a halt
in mid-air there demons who would be at me.

May fade before, sweet morning on sweet morning,
I wake my dreams, my fan-mail go astray,
and do me little goods I have not thought of,
ingenious & beneficial Father.

Ease in their passing my beloved friends,
all others too I have cared for in a travelling life,
anyone anywhere indeed. Lift up
sober toward truth a scared self-estimate.

FROM **OPUS DEI**

Lauds

Let us rejoice on our cots, for His nocturnal miracles
antique outside the Local Group & within it
& within our hearts in it, and for quotidian miracles
parsecs-off yielding to the Hale reflector.

Oh He is potent in the corners. Men
with Him are potent: quasars we intuit,
and sequent to sufficient discipline
we perceive this glow keeping His winter out.

My marvellous black new brim-rolled felt is both stuffy
    & raffish,
I hit my summit with it, in firelight.
Maybe I only got a Yuletide tie
(increasing sixty) & some writing-paper

but ha (ha*ha*) I've bought myself a hat!
Plus-strokes from position zero! Its feathers sprout.
Thank you, Your Benevolence!
permissive, smiling on   our silliness You forged.

Compline

I would at this late hour as little as may be
(in-negligent Father) plead. Not that I'm not attending,
only I kneel here spelled
under a mystery of one midnight

un-numbing now toward sorting in & out
I've got to get as little as possible wrong
O like Josiah then I heard with horror
instructions ancient as for the prime time

I am the king's son who squat down in rags
declared unfit by wise friends to inherit
and nothing of me left but skull & feet
& bloody among their dogs the palms of my hands.

Adorns my crossbar Your high frenzied Son,
mute over catcalls. How to conduct myself?
Does 'l'affabilité, l'humilité'
drift hither from the Jesuit wilderness,

a programme so ambitious? I am ambitious
but I have always stood content with towers
& traffic quashing thro' my canyons wild,
gunfire & riot fan out new Detroit.

Lord, long the day done—lapse, & by bootstraps,
oaths & toads, tranquil microseconds,
memory engulfing, odor of bacon burning
again—phantasmagoria prolix—

a rapture, though, of the Kingdom here here now
in the heart of a child—not far, nor hard to come by,
but natural as water falling, cupped
& lapped & slaking the child's dusty thirst!

If He for me as I feel for my daughter,
being His son, I'll sweat no more tonight
but happy hymn & sleep. I have got it made,
and so have all we of contrition, for

if He loves me He must love everybody
and Origen was right & Hell is empty
or will be at apocatastasis.
Sinners, sin on. We'll suffer now & later

but not forever, dear friends & brothers! Moreover:
my old Black freshman friend's mild formula
for the quarter-mile, 'I run the first 220
as fast as possible, to get out in front.

Then I run the second 220 even faster,
to stay out in front.' So may I run for You,
less laggard lately, less deluded man
of oxblood expectation
with fiery little resiny aftertastes.

Heard sapphire flutings. The winter will end.
        I remember You.
The sky was red. My pillow's cold & blanched.
There are no fair bells in this city. This fireless house
lies down at Your disposal as usual! Amen!

Washington in Love

I

Rectitude, and the terrible upstanding member

II

The music of our musketry is: *beautiful*

III

Intolerable Sally, loved in vain

IV

Mr Adams of Massachusetts . . . I accept, gentlemen.

V

Aloes. Adders. Roman gratitude.

VI

My porch elevation from the Potomac is 174′, 7½″.

VII

Bring the wounded, Martha! *Bring the wounded, men.*

Your Birthday in Wisconsin You Are 140

'One of the wits of the school' your chum would say—
Hot diggity!— What the *hell* went wrong for you,
Miss Emily,—besides the 'pure & terrible' Congressman
your paralyzing papa,—and Mr Humphrey's dying
      & Benjamin's the other reader? . . .

Fantastic at 32 outpour, uproar, 'terror
since September, I could tell to none'
after your 'Master' moved his family West
and timidly to Mr Higginson:
      'say if my verse is alive.'

Now you wore only white, now you did not appear,
till frantic 50 when you hurled your heart
down before Otis, who would none of it
thro' five years for 'Squire Dickinson's cracked daughter'
      awful by months, by hours . . .

Well. Thursday afternoon, I'm in W——
drinking your ditties, and (dear) *they* are *alive*,—
more so than (bless her) Mrs F who teaches
farmers' red daughters & their beaux *my* ditties
      and yours & yours & yours!
      Hot diggity!

He Resigns

Age, and the deaths, and the ghosts.
Her having gone away
in spirit from me. Hosts
of regrets come & find me empty.

I don't feel this will change.
I don't want any thing
or person, familiar or strange.
I don't think I will sing

any more just now;
or ever. I must start
to sit with a blind brow
above an empty heart.

FROM **Scherzo**

Henry by Night

Henry's nocturnal habits were the terror of his women.
First it appears he snored, lying on his back.
Then he thrashed & tossed,
changing position like a task fleet. Then, inhuman,
he woke every hour or so—they couldn't keep track
of mobile Henry, lost

at 3 a.m., off for more drugs or a cigarette,
reading old mail, writing new letters, scribbling
excessive Songs;
back then to bed, to the old tune or get set
for a stercoraceous cough, without quibbling
death-like. His women's wrongs

they hoarded & forgave, mysterious, sweet;
but you'll admit it was no way to live
or even keep alive.
I won't mention the dreams I won't repeat
sweating & shaking: something's gotta give:
up for good at five.

Henry's Understanding

He was reading late, at Richard's, down in Maine,
aged 32? Richard & Helen long in bed,
my good wife long in bed.
All I had to do was strip & get into my bed,
putting the marker in the book, & sleep,
& wake to a hot breakfast.

Off the coast was an island, P'tit Manaan,
the bluff from Richard's lawn was almost sheer.
A chill at four o'clock.
It only takes a few minutes to make a man.
A concentration upon now & here.
Suddenly, unlike Bach,

& horribly, unlike Bach, it occurred to me
that *one* night, instead of warm pajamas,
I'd take off all my clothes
& cross the damp cold lawn & down the bluff
into the terrible water & walk forever
under it out toward the island.

Defensio in Extremis

I said: Mighty men have encamped against me,
and they have questioned not only the skill of my
    defences
but my sincerity.
Now, Father, let them have it.

Thou knowest, whatever their outcry & roar,
in quietness I read my newly simple heart
after so far returning.
O even X, great Y, fine Z

splinter at my procedures and my ends.
Surely their spiritual life is not what it might be?
Surely they are half-full of it?
Tell them to leave me damned well alone with my
    insights.

Somber Prayer

O my Lord, I am not eloquent
neither heretofore, nor since Thou hast spoken . . .
but I am slow of speech, of a dim tongue.
He mentions, here, Thy 'counsel and dominion';

so I will borrow Newton's mouth. Spare me
Uccello's ark-locked lurid deluge, I'm
the brutal oaf from the barrel stuck mid-scene,—
or ghost me past the waters . . . Miriam . . .

A twelve-year-old all solemn, sorry-faced,
described himself lately as 'a lifetime prick.'
Me too. Maladaptive devices.
At fifty-five half-famous & effective, I still feel rotten
    about myself.

Panicky weekdays, I pray hard,
not worthy.
Sucking, clinging, following, crying, smiling,
I come Your child to You.

Overseas Prayer

Good evening. At the feet of the king, my Lord,
I fall seven & yet seven times.
Behold what insult has Your servant suffered
from Shuwardata and Milkiln & his ilk.

Put them under saws, & under harrows of iron,
& under axes of iron, make them pass thro' the
    brick-kiln
lest at any time they flirt at me again.
Enjoin them to the blurred & breathless dead.

The Valley of the Cheesemakers has disappeared
also, my Lord. Your precincts are in ruin,
your revenues ungathered. Minarets
blot our horizon as I pen, my Lord.

I feel myself a deep & old objection.
You gave me not a very able father,
joyless at last, Lord, and sometimes I hardly
(thinking on him) perform my duty to you.

Ah then I mutter 'Forty-odd years past.
Do I yet repine?' and go about your business,—
a fair wind and the honey lights of home
being all I ask this wind-torn foreign evening.

Certainty Before Lunch

Ninety percent of the mass of the Universe
(90%!) may be gone in collapsars,
pulseless, lightless, forever, if they exist.
My friends the probability man & I

& his wife the lawyer are taking a country walk
in the flowerless April snow in exactly two hours
and maybe won't be back. Finite & unbounded
the massive spirals absolutely fly

distinctly apart, by math *and* observation,
current math, this morning's telescopes
& inference. My wife is six months gone
so won't be coming. That mass must be somewhere!

or not? just barely possibly *may not*
BE anywhere? My Lord, I'm glad we don't
on x or y depend for Your being there.
I know You are there. The sweat is, I am here.

'How Do You Do, Dr Berryman, Sir?'

Edgy, perhaps. *Not* on the point of bursting-forth,
but toward that latitude,—I think? *Not* 'shout loud &
      march straight.'
Each lacks something in some direction. I
am not entirely at the mercy of.

The tearing of hair no.

Pickt up pre-dawn & tortured and detained,
Mr Tan Mam and many other students
sit tight but vocal in illegal cells
and as for Henry Pussycat   he'd just as soon be dead

(on the Promise of—I know it sounds incredible—
if can he muster penitence enough—
he can't though—
glory)

King David Dances

Aware to the dry throat of the wide hell in the world,
O trampling empires, and mine one of them,
and mine one gross desire against His sight,
slaughter devising there,
some good behind, ambiguous ahead,
revolted sons, a pierced son, bound to bear,
mid hypocrites amongst idolaters,
mockt in abysm by one shallow wife,
with the ponder both of priesthood & of State
heavy upon me, yea,
all the black same I dance my blue head off!

BIOGRAPHICAL NOTE

NOTE ON THE TEXTS

NOTES

INDEX OF TITLES &
FIRST LINES

BIOGRAPHICAL NOTE

John Berryman was born October 25, 1914, in McAlester, Oklahoma. He graduated from Columbia University in 1936, and did graduate work at Cambridge, where he was an Oldham Shakespeare Scholar, and at Princeton University, where he was a Creative Writing Fellow. He taught at Wayne State University (1939), Princeton (1940–43), Harvard (1945–49), University of Washington (1950), and University of Cincinnati (1951–52); from 1954 to 1972 he was a member of the English department of the University of Minnesota, becoming a full professor. His awards included the Shelley Memorial Award (1949), the Levinson Prize (1950), the Harriet Monroe Award (1957) for *Homage to Mistress Bradstreet*, the Pulitzer Prize (1964) for *77 Dream Songs*, and the National Book Award for *His Toy, His Dream, His Rest* (1968). In addition to his numerous books of poetry, he was also the author of the biography *Stephen Crane* (1950), essays and short stories collected posthumously in *The Freedom of the Poet* (1976), an unfinished novel about his long struggle with alcoholism, *Recovery* (1973), and various writings on Shakespeare published as *Berryman's Shakespeare* in 1999. He took his own life on January 7, 1972.

NOTE ON THE TEXTS

In general, this volume prints the texts of poems as they were first published in one of John Berryman's books. For uncollected poems, this volume prints texts published in periodicals or anthologies. The sources for the texts of the poems, grouped by the sectional divisions in this volume, are listed below.

Early Poems 1935–1942. The texts of the poems in this section are taken from the following sources: "Note on E. A. Robinson": Joseph Auslander et al. (eds.), *Columbia Poetry 1935* (New York: Columbia University Press, 1935); "Elegy: Hart Crane": Allan Abbott et al. (eds.), *Columbia Poetry 1936* (New York: Columbia University Press, 1936); "The Second Cactus" and "Prague": James Laughlin, ed., *New Directions in Prose & Poetry 1939* (Norfolk, CT: New Directions, 1939); "The Apparition" and "The Curse": John Berryman, "Twenty Poems" in *Five Young American Poets* (Norfolk, CT: New Directions, 1940); "To Bhain Campbell" and "Epilogue": John Berryman, *Poems* (Norfolk, CT: New Directions, 1942).

From *The Dispossessed*. The texts of the poems in this section are taken from *The Dispossessed* (New York: William Sloane Associates, 1948).

Homage to Mistress Bradstreet. This poem was first published in *Partisan Review* in 1953. The text printed here is taken from *Homage to Mistress Bradstreet* (New York: Farrar, Straus & Cudahy, 1956).

From *Berryman's Sonnets*. All but seven of the sonnets in the sequence published in 1967 as *Berryman's Sonnets* were originally written in 1947 (of the sonnets included here, 107, 112, 113, 114, and 115 were written in 1966, as was the prefatory poem). When preparing *Berryman's Sonnets* for publication, Berryman changed proper names (most significantly, "Chris" in earlier versions was changed to "Lise") and made other revisions. The texts of the poems in this section are taken from their first book publication, *Berryman's Sonnets* (New York: Farrar, Straus and Giroux, 1967).

From *His Thought Made Pockets & the Plane Buckt* (1958). The texts of the poems in this section are taken from *His Thought Made Pockets & the Plane Buckt* (Pawlet, VT: Claude Fredericks, 1958).

Poems 1950–1964. The texts of the poems in this section are taken from the following sources: "The Will" and "Waiting" [from "The Black Book"]: *Poetry*, January 1950; Of Isaac Rosenfeld: *Partisan Review*, Fall 1956; Formal Elegy: John Berryman, *Short Poems* (New York: Farrar, Straus and Giroux, 1967).

From The Dream Songs. Berryman's long sequence *The Dream Songs* was published in two separate books—*77 Dream Songs* (1964) and *His Toy, His Dream, His Rest* (1968)—before being collected in a single volume, *The Dream Songs*, in 1969. The present volume prints the texts of the poems in this sequence from their first book publication, either from *77 Dream Songs* (New York: Farrar, Straus and Company, 1964) or *His Toy, His Dream, His Rest* (New York: Farrar, Straus and Giroux, 1968).

From *Love & Fame* (1970). Texts of the poems in this section are taken from *Love & Fame* (New York: Farrar, Straus and Giroux, 1970).

From *Delusions, Etc.* (1972). Texts of the poems in this section are taken from *Delusions, Etc.* (New York: Farrar, Straus and Giroux, 1972).

This volume presents the texts of the original printings chosen for inclusion here, but it does not attempt to reproduce nontextual features of their typographic design. Spelling, punctuation, and capitalization are often expressive features and are not altered, even when inconsistent or irregular. The texts are presented without change, except for the correction of typographical errors: 136.6, dissheveled; 143.17, better,'; 165.8, parsees-off.

NOTES

7.1   Bhain Campbell]   Poet and friend of Berryman who died of cancer in 1940 at the age of 29. His only book of poems, *The Task*, was published in 1945. The following poem, "Epilogue," and "A Poem for Bhain" (p. 18) are also about Campbell.

11.12   Che si cruccia,]   From Dante's question to Virgil in Canto XIX of *Inferno*: "Chi è colui, maestro, che si cruccia / guizzando più che li altri suoi consorti . . ." (Master, who is that shade who suffers and quivers more than all his other comrades . . .)

16.1   1 September 1939]   The date of the German invasion of Poland, as well as a reference to Auden's poem "September 1, 1939."

17.2   the night of the Belgian surrender]   Over the opposition of his cabinet, King Leopold III of Belgium surrendered unconditionally to Germany on May 28, 1940.

18.4–5   treachery . . . Begun]   In 1936, Leopold had announced the abandonment of Belgium's alliance with France in favor of a policy of neutrality.

23.8   'That deep romantic chasm']   From Coleridge, "Kubla Khan" (1798).

23.11   'A poet . . . men']   Cf. Wordsworth's preface to *Lyrical Ballads* (1798).

26.19   Sweet . . . arrive]   In a prefatory note to *The Dispossessed*, Berryman wrote that this line is taken "from the great mad poem of Smart," i.e., Christopher Smart's "A Song to David" (1763).

28.1   *On m'analyse*]   They analyze me.

28.1–2   Kinsey / Shortly will tell us]   Alfred C. Kinsey (1894–1956) established the Institute for Sex Research at the University of Indiana in 1947; the first volume of his research, *Sexual Behavior in the Human Male* (popularly known as the Kinsey Report), was published the following year.

52.3–5   *a thousand years ago . . . publish them?*]   Most of the sonnets published in *Berryman's Sonnets* in 1967 were written 20 years earlier.

52.17   *Jacques Maritain says*]   In writings such as *Art et scholasticisme* (*Art and Scholasticism*, 1920), Catholic French philosopher Jacques Maritain (1882–1973) explored the relationship between theology and art.

54.14   once I lit Yeats']   Berryman met Yeats in London in 1937, when they had taken tea together.

54.16   Dylan]   Dylan Thomas.

63.9   Laertes' winding-sheet . . . night]   In Homer's *Odyssey*, Penelope wove a shroud for Ithacan king Laertes as a way of putting off her suitors. She claimed that she would choose one of her suitors when the shroud was finished but each night unraveled the previous day's work.

65.7   Sundam Trench]   The Sunda Trench, also known as the Java Trench, is a deep depression in the eastern Indian Ocean.

67.9   'Faire . . . Haire']   From the sonnet (1616) beginning "The sun is fair when he with crimson crown," by William Drummond of Hawthornden (1585–1649).

72.4   'Death . . . beauty.']   From Wallace Stevens, "Sunday Morning" (1923).

73.26–74.1   Endymion's Glaucus . . . sighed]   Book III of Keats' *Endymion* (1818) contains a free adaptation of the Greek legend of Glaucus and his beloved water-nymph Scylla, who was given a fatal potion by Circe. After a thousand years, with Endymion's help, Scylla is restored to life (along with a drowned multitude of "lovers lost" referred to at 73.27).

83.7–8   Tristan's . . . mistress]   In 1871, fleeing Paris under the Commune, Count Rodolphe de Battine and his mistress, the Italian actress Armida-Josefina Cuchiani, settled in Brittany for several months. There they met the poet Tristan Corbière, who fell in love with Cuchiani and wrote despairingly about her (as "Marcelle") in his sole collection of poetry, *Les amours jaunes* (*The Yellow Loves*, 1873). Berryman reviewed an English translation of Corbière's poems in 1947, while writing the sequence later published as *Berryman's Sonnets*.

83.18   'La Cuchiani . . . mais . .']   Cuchiani loved Tristan, but . . .

84.24   Tetélestai.]   "It is finished"—Christ's last words.

88.1   The Black Book]   A series of poems about the Holocaust that was never completed. In a 1966 interview Berryman commented: "I wrote about eight parts, I guess. It was in the form of a Mass for the Dead. It was designed to have 42 sections, and was about the Nazi murderers of the Jews. But I found I just couldn't take it. The sections published— there were eight of them in *Poetry*—are unrelievedly horrible. I wasn't able at the time—that was almost twenty years ago—to find any way of making palatable the monstrosity of the thing which obsessed me."

90.1   Wang Wei]   T'ang Dynasty poet and painter (699–759).

90.12   'freedom . . . matters.']   See the opening of Wang Wei's "Answering Vice-Prefect Zhang" in Witter Bynner's translation: "As the years go by, give me but peace, / Freedom from ten thousand matters."

93.1   Isaac Rosenfeld]   Critic, editor, and fiction writer (1918–1956), author of the novel *Passage from Home* (1946).

93.26–94.1   Ruby . . . testifying]   Jack Ruby claimed that he murdered Lee Harvey Oswald so Jacqueline Kennedy would not have to testify in Oswald's trial.

94.6   Patrolman Tippit]   J. D. Tippit, Dallas policeman who was shot when he approached Lee Harvey Oswald to question him on the afternoon of Kennedy's assassination.

102.8   Roethke]   Poet Theodore Roethke died on August 1, 1963, after collapsing in a neighbor's swimming pool on Bainbridge Island in Puget Sound. Berryman wrote this elegy the following week.

104.12   Joe]   Senator Joseph McCarthy.

104.12-13   Strauss . . . use] J. Robert Oppenheimer, the physicist who directed the design of the first atomic bombs at Los Alamos, 1943–45, had his security clearance revoked by the Atomic Energy Commission in 1954 after being accused of disloyalty. One of his bitter enemies was the chairman of the commission, Lewis Strauss.

104.13-14   Robb . . . Goldfine] Lawyer Roger Robb served as special counsel to the Atomic Energy Commision during its hearings regarding Oppenheimer's activities. He later represented the industrialist Bernard Goldfine during a congressional investigation of gifts Goldfine sent to Sherman Adams, Eisenhower's chief of staff.

104.17   Monty's memoirs] Field Marshall Bernard L. Montgomery (1887–1976) commanded British troops in northwest Europe, 1944–45, and disagreed with Eisenhower over strategy. He published several memoirs.

104.21   Adlai mine] Adlai Stevenson, who ran against Eisenhower in 1952 and 1956.

108.17   Between the Ices (Mindel-Würm)] "Kansan-Mindel" and "Wisconsin-Würm" are two of the major glacial advances that occurred during the last Ice Age.

112.2   Death . . . expert] Cf. Paul Celan's poem "Todesfugue" ("Death-fugue"), with its recurring phrase "der Tod ist ein Meister aus Deutschland" ("Death is a master from Germany").

114.6   *Do, ut des.*] I give, that you may give.

117.5–7   Gottfried Benn . . . win.] Cf. Benn's essay "Artists and Old Age": "Your art has deserted the temples and the sacrificial vessels, it has ceased to have anything to do with the painting of pillars, and the painting of chapels is no longer anything for you either. You are using your own skin for wallpaper, and nothing can save you."

117.24–25   Issa] Japanese poet Kobayashi Issa (1763–1827).

125.15   Walt's 'orbic flex,'] See Whitman, *Song of Myself*, section 26: "A tenor large and fresh as the creation fills me, / The orbic flex of his mouth is pouring and filling me full."

130.10   Delmore] Poet Delmore Schwartz was found dead in a Manhattan hotel in July 1966 after he disappeared for several weeks.

130.23   Gertrude] Schwartz's first wife.

132.20   'An Ancient to Ancients']   Poem (1922) by Thomas Hardy.

134.7–9   he seized Ted . . . Plath]   Theodore Roethke (see note 102.8); the poet and critic R. P. Blackmur, who died because of a heart ailment on February 2, 1965; poet Randall Jarrell was struck and killed by an automobile on October 14, 1965; poet Sylvia Plath committed suicide on February 11, 1963.

146.1   Ralph Hodgson]   English lyric poet (1871–1962) who spent much of his life in Japan and, after 1940, on a farm in Ohio living in near-seclusion.

147.16   McGovern]   Tom McGovern, Berryman's classmate at Columbia.

148.5   'Elegy: Hart Crane']   See pp. 1–3.

148.19   the Trials]   Three public show trials were held in Moscow in August 1936, January 1937, and March 1938, during which prominent Soviet Communists were falsely accused of conspiring with the exiled Leon Trotsky against Joseph Stalin and his regime.

149.16   'Puppet-theatre']   Kleist's 1811 essay "Über das Marionet-tentheater" ("On the Puppet Theater").

150.8–9   Tom . . . Willie]   T. S. Eliot, James Joyce, and William Faulkner.

152.7   McLuhan & Frye]   Canadian media theorist Marshall McLuhan (1911–1980), author of *The Gutenberg Galaxy* (1962) and *Understanding Media* (1964); Canadian structuralist literary critic Northrop Frye (1912–1991), author of *Anatomy of Criticism* (1957).

154.8   Malcolm Lowry's book]   The novel *Under the Volcano* (1947).

159.2–4   John Jacob Niles . . . earlier-78 recordings]   The recording career of the American folk singer, composer, and folklorist John Jacob Niles (1892–1980) began with the compilations *Early American Ballads* (1938) and *Early American Carols and Folksongs* (1940), released by RCA.

160.16   Kate]   Berryman's wife.

165.6   Local Group]   Comprising more than 30 galaxies, the Local Group includes the Andromeda Galaxy and the Milky Way (Earth's galaxy).

165.8   the Hale reflector]   One of the world's most powerful telescopes, housed at the Palomar Observatory in San Diego County, California.

166.7–8   as little . . . Josiah]   Josiah, biblical king of Judah in the 7th century B.C.E., is praised for doing "that which was right in the sight of the Lord" (2 Kings 22.2).

168.19–20   'pure & terrible' Congressman . . . papa]   Shortly after the death of her father in 1874, Emily Dickinson wrote to Thomas Wentworth Higginson, "His heart was pure and terrible and I think no other like it exists." Edward Dickinson had served as a Massachusetts state senator and a member of the U.S. House of Representatives.

168.20   Mr. Humphrey's dying]   Dickinson's friend Leonard Humphrey died of brain fever in 1850, at the age of 26.

168.21   Benjamin's]   Benjamin Franklin Newton, who encouraged Dickinson as a writer and to whom she sent some of her poems, shortly before his death in 1853.

169.1–2   'terror . . . none']   From a letter to Higginson dated April 25, 1862.

169.3   'Master' . . . West]   The Rev. Charles Wadsworth, the Presbyterian minister whom Dickinson once referred to as her "closest earthly friend," moved with his family to San Francisco in 1862. The person addressed as "Master" by Dickinson in three letters and seven poems may be Wadsworth.

169.5   'say . . . alive.']   From a letter to Higginson dated April 15, 1862.

169.8   Otis]   Lawyer and Massachusetts Supreme Court justice Otis Phillips Lord, to whom Dickinson wrote love letters. Lord's portion of their correspondence has not survived.

169.9   'Squire . . . daughter']   Cf. Higginson's letter to his sister Anna, December 28, 1876, referring to "my partially cracked poetess at Amherst."

171.8   Richard's]   The poet and critic R. P. Blackmur.

172.20–21   Thy 'counsel . . . Newton's mouth.]   See Newton, *Principia* (1687): "This most beautiful system of the sun, planets, and comets could only proceed from the counsel and dominion of an intelligent and powerful Being."

172.22   Uccello's . . . deluge]   Paulo Uccello's fresco *The Deluge* (ca. 1450), in the Green Cloister of the Santa Maria Novella church in Florence.

173.14   Shuwardata and Milkiln]   The El-Amarna letters, 14th-century B.C.E. cuneiform tablets discovered in Egypt in 1887, refer to the conquests of Shuwardata, prince of Hebron, and Milkilu, prince of Gezer.

173.20   Valley of the Cheesemakers]   Tyropoeon Valley, Josephus' name for the valley that in antiquity separated the upper city of Jerusalem from the Temple. It has since been filled in.

INDEX OF TITLES
AND FIRST LINES

ABOUT THIS SERIES

The American Poets Project offers, for the first time in our history, a compact national library of American poetry. Selected and introduced by distinguished poets and scholars, elegant in design and textually authoritative, the series makes widely available the full scope of our poetic heritage.

For other titles in the American Poets Project, or for information on subscribing to the series, please visit: www.americanpoetsproject.org.

ABOUT THE PUBLISHER

The Library of America, a nonprofit publisher, is dedicated to preserving America's best and most significant writing in handsome, enduring volumes, featuring authoritative texts. For a free catalog, to subscribe to the series, or to learn how you can help support The Library's mission, please visit www.loa.org or write: The Library of America, 14 East 60th Street, New York, NY 10022.

AMERICAN POETS PROJECT